Penny Stocks Trading for Beginners: 3-Hour Crash Course

Build Passive Income While Investing From Home

Edward Day

Table of Contents

Introduction

"Markets are never wrong — opinions often are." - Jesse Livermore

How would you like to make a million dollars? Well, of course you would! One of the reasons you picked up this book is probably because you heard of the enormous potential penny stocks have when it comes to increasing the size of your wealth. This curiosity has led you to study more about this topic.

Financial markets have been one of the biggest creators of wealth in America over the past century. Over the years many ambitious people have been attracted to them in the hopes of making a large amount of money. However, the sad truth is that many of these people don't do well.

A study conducted by brokers reveals that over 90% of traders end up losing their entire trading capital within a year of opening their accounts (Rodriguez & Rodriguez, 2016). Why does trading have such a high failure rate? What is it about the markets that causes intelligent people to lose money like this?

More importantly, what do the 10% do that the other 90% don't? Do these 10 percenters have special knowledge? Well, yes and no. They have special knowledge in the sense that they've figured out how to think about the markets in an intelligent manner. Otherwise, they're no different from any one of us.

All they've done is learn the right way to do things. You too can learn these methods and achieve the success that they have experienced. I must warn you, though. This is not a book that will teach you a get-rich-quick scheme. My personal belief is that such schemes only result in tears.

In this book, I'm going to introduce you to a powerful asset class that exists in the market. I'll give you the tools needed to trade them well. I'll also show you how you can unearth them easily. Finally, I'll show you how you can go about analyzing them and place intelligent trades.

While I'll show you everything, it's still up to you to go ahead and place trades. You'll need to do your homework and work hard to find these opportunities. You can't expect someone else to do all the work for you and you cannot expect this money to come to you easily.

When it comes to trading, the person that works the hardest wins the most. The markets don't care about your background or your education level. They do care about the amount of work you're willing to put in and it rewards those who have done their homework.

This is the task that lies ahead of you. So having said that, why should you choose to trade penny stocks? What makes them so special?

Rewards and Time Invested

Let's say you have two investment opportunities. They both require you to spend equal amounts of time on them. The difference is that one pays you a 10% return while the other pays you 200%. Which one would you choose?

The second opportunity is a no-brainer in this case! If you need to spend a lot of time working on an opportunity, it makes sense to get paid as much as possible! This is what differentiates penny stocks from other trading instruments such as regular stocks and Forex.

Let's say you decide to trade the stock of Amazon, which is priced north of $1,500. If this stock moves $20, that's a 1.3% move. This is significant. If you managed to capture that gain in a day, you'd have had a decent trading session.

Now compare this another stock that is priced at $1. Let's say this stock moved by 50 cents. This is a far smaller move numerically but in percentage terms, it's huge. It's actually a 50% move. Which move would you rather capture? A 50% move or a 1.3% one?

The great thing about this is the amount of work you need to perform in order to realize your gain in each opportunity is exactly the same. There is no different set of rules by which the stock of Amazon plays by compared to the penny stock. Both of them are subject to market forces and both of them attract short-term speculators and long-term investors alike.

It's just that one moves far more than the other in percentage terms despite moving far less in numerical terms. When it comes to trading success, percentage returns are what you want to be focusing on. A $20 move that makes you just one percent is far inferior to a 50 cent move that makes you 50%.

Penny stocks have given traders around the world the ability to turn capital of under $1,000 into five and even six figures. This is because it takes a very small move for the trader to realize a huge percentage profit.

Many traders view such numbers and enter the market without giving a second thought to things such as risk management and proper screening. This is what consigns them to the 90% category of unsuccessful traders I mentioned earlier. While it's great that you want to make lots of money, you should not expect it to be served up to you on a platter.

If you're willing to work hard for it, it'll come to you in droves. This is something I'm quite familiar with, via my own trading career.

My Story

Mine isn't the sort of rags-to-riches story you hear about from most trading gurus. In fact, I had a pretty sedate start. I was always intrigued by finance and the markets, and studied accounting in college. After graduating, I got myself a steady job as a chartered accountant. By every measure, I had a stable and successful life.

However, the markets kept calling me and I felt that I wasn't achieving my full potential. It just so happened that one of my clients was a full-time Forex trader. He invited me to a seminar on Forex trading and it didn't take long for me to get completely hooked.

I started working on my Forex trading skills; in 2008 I was fortunate enough to be able to quit my regular job and trade Forex full-time. While I am a full-time Forex trader, I have traded stocks, options and futures over the years. The markets are where I make my money and it is how I provide for my family.

Aside from the markets, I'm also a frequent guest speaker on the Forex trading circuit and I even mentor a few people to help them achieve their dreams. If there's anything that underlines my story, it's that managing risk and setting realistic goals have helped me more than anything else.

I'm here to tell you that the astronomical returns you find most trading gurus talking about are possible for you to achieve. However, you're not going to get there overnight. With patience and perseverance, you too will be able to call yourself a successful penny stock trader. You'll have the life you want and the amount of money that you've dreamed of earning.

You'll need to work for it, of course. As I said, this money isn't going to come to you for free. There will be times when you'll feel like throwing the towel in. Always remember why you're doing this and why the money you're looking to make is important to you. This will ensure you never lack motivation.

Now that you're ready to begin your penny stock journey, let's dive into the basics of what they are!

Chapter 1:

Penny Stocks 101

So, what are penny stocks anyway? Do they really cost just a penny?

Penny stocks is the phrase used to describe all stocks in the market that are traded for less than $5 per share. There's a huge difference between $5 and a penny, of course! Historically, the stocks that were almost worthless, or that represented companies that were small and insignificant, traded for a penny.

Over the years, as the market grew in size and trading volumes increased, the category of penny stocks expanded to where it is today. Penny stocks represent companies that are small and don't make huge news waves. These stocks are also referred to as being micro caps or small caps.

A company's market capitalization or market cap is calculated by multiplying the number of shares it has outstanding by the price of each share. Companies that are less than $300 million in size are referred to as micro caps. Small caps are between $300 million and one billion in size.

The small cap companies that are on the lower end of that scale often have shares trading for prices less than $5. These stocks are often deemed risky to trade for a variety of reasons. Either the companies they represent are far too small and unstable, or they don't disclose enough financial information for investors and traders to form an informed opinion.

For this reason, small and micro cap stocks have often been deemed too risky to trade. You'll hear a lot about how penny stock trading is risky and that the average person ought to stay away from them. This is true. You need to do your homework before jumping into trading them.

However, this also happens to be true of any type of asset you wish to trade. If you don't understand how it works, how can you hope to be successful? The fact is that when you trade stocks, your holding times are not going to be as long as they are when you're investing for the long-term.

An investor seeks to hold their shares for close to a decade. With such timelines in place, obviously a lot could go wrong with a small company. With trading, your longest holding time is going to be a few days to a week at the most. If you've done your homework and have used the screening strategies I'll show you in this book, you won't have to worry about unexpected events ruining your trades.

If the amount of work you need to put into analyzing regular stocks is the same as the work you put into analyzing penny stocks, and if the risks associated with them are the same over the short-term, then why not go with the asset that can appreciate a lot more?

This, in short, is the reasoning behind trading penny stocks. Small moves lead to gargantuan gains for the trader. As a result, your capital compounds faster and you get paid a lot more for doing the same amount of work as with the other options out there.

Not all penny stocks are created equal. As you've just learned, in the case of some of them there's a very good reason they're selling for a few pennies. All penny stocks can be classified into tiers. These tiers will inform you of the risks associated with trading them and you'll be able to make trading decisions easily.

Tiers

One of the biggest negatives of the large majority of penny stocks is that they're open to manipulation. If you're even remotely interested in the market, you've probably heard of the story of the con man Jordan Belfort. Belfort's name often comes up alongside penny stocks and this has led to all penny stocks being tarnished.

Belfort and his cronies ran a scheme called the pump and dump. The way it works is that the con artist buys a large block of stock in the company and then sells it to outside investors. As the demand increases, so does the price and the con artist sells all of their shares.

In such schemes, a stock selling for 50 cents can be pumped up to $2 or $3 and then dumped in the market. Once the hype stops and the large block of shares have been sold, the price slides right back down to 50 cents or so.

Pump and dumps continue to exist these days and avoiding the stocks that attract such schemes should be your first step. The classification of penny stocks into tiers aims to help you do just that.

Tier One

This is where you should be focusing your attention the most. These stocks sell for around $5 or slightly more. The price isn't as important as is the market they trade on. Tier One penny stocks trade on reputed exchanges like the New York Stock Exchange (NYSE) or the National Securities Dealers Automated Quotations (NASDAQ).

The NYSE and NASDAQ, and indeed any major stock exchange, has a variety of rules in place to prevent investors and traders from being defrauded. All the stocks that trade on these markets are subject to strict regulation by the Securities and Exchange Commission (SEC).

The SEC in turn mandates that all companies on the exchange file annual, quarterly and half-yearly financial reports. They're also required to file a series of documents that prove they haven't been engaging in insider trading. Insider trading is the term given to a scenario where the company management secretly buys stock without disclosing it.

After all, the managers are privy to information that the general public isn't. The SEC has mandated that managers can place trades, but they're required to immediately disclose this information. This way, the information advantage is smoothed out to a large extent. The public comes to know of such purchases (or sales) the minute they happen.

In addition to this, the financial statements of these companies are also required to adhere to Generally Accepted Accounting Principles or GAAP. GAAP is a framework that governs all corporate accounting. It isn't without its flaws, but given the large number of industries it has to apply to, it's the best system we have.

GAAP has strict criteria in place for important accounting items such as revenue recognition. Smaller companies are often tempted to play fast and loose with this. They might recognize a signed memorandum of understanding as proof of revenue or payment. Such practices are outlawed under GAAP.

The penalties for violating these rules are huge. Managers and associated stock promoters (usually a bank) face jail time and heavy fines if they cross the line. More damaging is the fact that their reputation takes a blow, and they'll typically never recover from it.

As a result, there's zero incentive for anyone to break the rules. A listing on the NYSE or NASDAQ is a point of pride and all companies do their best to adhere to the listing requirements. There are other reputable stock exchanges as well such as the BATS, NYSE ARCA and IEX.

If you're just starting out, stick to these exchanges and don't stray from them. Many experienced penny stock traders stick to such instruments, and they do very well for themselves. So it isn't as if you ever need to leave this tier to make money.

Tier Two

These stocks are in a gray area. Typically, they're priced below a dollar and are still listed on a reputable exchange. However, they're in danger of falling foul of listing regulations. Such companies receive an official notice from the exchange notifying them of this condition, along with remedial steps they need to carry out.

This notice is made public so you'll be able to access this information the minute it is issued. The delisting process varies from one company to the next. The most common reason for Tier Two stocks to fall foul of the exchange is that their trading price closed below a dollar for 30 consecutive days (Bloomenthal, 2020).

Once this happens, the initials 'BC' are appended to the stock ticker (the symbol of the stock. AMZN is Amazon's ticker) so everyone knows that the stock is under probation. An official notice is sent to the company requesting them to take remedial measures. The company might get in touch with a stock promoter to drum up some positive publicity to drive prices over a dollar again.

Once the notice is received, the company has 10 business days to respond with a plan of action. If they fail to do this, the stock will be delisted from the exchange. This process takes around one working week. All shareholders will have to be notified and your broker will give you a notice with regard to this process.

You can continue to hold on to your position, but given that the company is moving away from a major market, you'll be unlikely to find other people to trade with. As a result, most investors sell their shares immediately, which further drives prices down.

If the company's remedial plan is accepted by the exchange, they have another few weeks to put it into place. The time provided by the exchange for remedial action is actually defined by the company itself, in their plan of action. If the issue is addressed, then the stock continues trading.

If you've been following along, you'll notice that there is a straightforward trade here. A stock that is priced below a dollar with the initials BC is likely to increase to above a dollar since this is what preserves its listing status. This is a good screen for penny stocks. You'll have to perform some further homework on the stock itself, but it's a good way to narrow your field of play.

Most stocks that receive notices fail to comply with requirements within their remedial periods. This means the stocks that do comply tend to receive an even bigger price boost. After all, every other trader out there jumps into it if the probability of it complying is high.

This increases demand and prices move higher as a result. Despite the bullish case for Tier Two stocks being present, beginners are best served by staying away from them. It takes experience to spot a good Tier Two stock and you stand to lose money if you're incorrect.

Even worse, you'll be stuck with a stock that doesn't trade and you won't be able to exit your position in it.

Tier Three

These are the Belfort type stocks. It's a reflection of how risky penny stocks can be that even a prolific con artist stayed away from the bottom tier of stocks. Stocks in Tier Three do not trade in major exchanges. Instead, they trade Over The Counter or OTC. These stocks are also referred to as pink sheets.

Back in the day, before the markets became fully electronic, the exchanges used to have physical order desks. Investors and traders could walk up and buy a stock that was listed on the exchange. They were given a sheet that denoted the price they had bought or sold the stock at and this sheet was proof of ownership until the stock certificate arrived in the mail. It served as a receipt, in short.

Stocks that didn't trade on the major exchanges could be bought from trade desks situated outside the confines of the exchange, in smaller trading houses. These stocks didn't have a listed price and the price you paid depended on how well you could negotiate.

If the seller gave you a price of a dollar but you said 50 cents and if they accepted your offer, this counted as a sale. The investor or trader would be handed a sheet in this case as well. However, since it wasn't a listed stock, this sheet would be pink. Hence, the name, pink sheets.

These days all trade desks are electronic so there's no physical sheet that you receive. However, there isn't much of a market for pink sheets. You can view their prices on your trading software, but they won't move much. When they do move, it'll probably be abrupt.

What's more, their price spread will be huge. I'll explain the concept of the spread in the next chapter. For now, just understand that you want the spread to be as small as possible. A huge spread reduces the probability of making a profit on the trade.

OTC markets are not fully governed by the SEC and aren't subject to the same laws as the regulated exchanges are. Truth be told, the SEC stipulations are not enforced uniformly in these markets. In order to succeed you need to have a lot of insider information on the stock, or a large amount of capital in order to move prices and sway the market.

Not all OTC markets are bad. There are some legitimate companies that can be found here. In addition to this, the bond derivatives market, which happens to be the second largest in the world after Forex, is an OTC market. Prices are negotiated for hundreds of millions of dollars' worth of bonds and other fixed income instruments.

Thus, OTC by itself doesn't mean fraud or unreliability. It just so happens that the OTC stock markets have these characteristics. Stay far away from such stocks.

Tier Four

These stocks are usually priced under a cent or close to it. They trade in fractional quantities and are often the subject of 'hot stock' newsletters. Almost every single one of them is subject to fraud of some kind. These days, it's tough to run pump and dump schemes from the United States or any developed economy.

Scammers turn to offshore jurisdictions such as Belize or Cyprus and buy large quantities of these stocks. They push newsletters out to gullible people and have the price pumped up to a cent or two cents.

This results in windfalls of more than 2000% for them and once they sell their holdings, the price of the stock falls right back down.

Needless to say, stay away from such newsletters and stocks.

Regulations

As I've mentioned previously you should stick to stocks that trade on the major exchanges. This provides you with a lot of security and you're not going to fall prey to a fraudulent scheme. Having said that, you still need to do a lot of homework before you can successfully trade such stocks.

If you're trading on these exchanges, you are going to be subject to a few rules and regulations. All participants in these markets have to adhere to the rules that pertain to them. Market participants include traders, brokers and clearing houses. Clearing houses won't impact your trading in any way, so I'm not going to discuss them. Good brokers choose reputable clearing houses, so all you need to do is find such a broker.

Brokerage houses are regulated by the Financial Regulation Authority (FINRA). FINRA administers pretty much every professional operating in the markets and runs a large number of licensing exams. For example, your broker and all of their employees need to pass these exams in order to be certified to operate in the markets.

Brokers are an important factor when it comes to your trading success. It's worthwhile taking some time to understand how they operate.

Brokers

People who are new to the markets often view their brokers as being market experts. The fact is that your broker has no clue about the markets any more than you do. This mistake often stems from the fact that the broker is the one providing access to the market. This leads new investors/traders to believe that since they have access, they must be experts.

It's a lot like asking the guy who opens the doors to an expensive building what the real estate prospects of a neighborhood are. He can probably tell you something about who lives there and a few other tidbits. But is he really the person you want to be relying on?

It's the same with brokers and the markets. Their job is to execute your trades as reliably as possible and for the best prices they can find in the market. Their employees are licensed on their ability to do this. Thus, asking them for trading advice is nonsensical. You might as well ask a random person on the street, for all the good it does.

Many people evaluate brokers on the basis of the trading advice they provide or the recommendations they give. This is the worst possible way of evaluating their services. In fact, brokers that tout the quality of their recommendations are usually the worst sort. This is because their aim is to attract people who know nothing about the markets.

Brokers that cater to professional traders only highlight their quality of execution and the finer points of their trading software. If you wish to be successful, you need to focus on these things as well. Don't expect someone else to make trading decisions for you. Do your homework and trust your ability to make the right choices.

What should you look for in a broker? The first point to note is whether they're registered with FINRA. The longer they've been registered, the better. You also want to choose brokers that are registered in the continental United States. The SEC and FINRA do have a list of registered foreign brokers but it's hard to see any advantage that these brokers provide.

Some examples of good brokers are:

1. Lightspeed Trading - This platform is designed for active traders. You will pay commissions on your trades depending on the volumes you buy or sell.
2. Robinhood - Everyone's favorite app! Robinhood offers zero commission trades. However, there is a catch that I'll shortly discuss. This makes the app less suited for traders that have large account balances or trade large positions.

3. TradeStation - One of the most respected brokers in the trading space. This should be your default choice.
4. Interactive Brokers - The best brokers for advanced traders. IB offers access to international markets for low cost. The platform has a learning curve to it but once up to speed, it's easy to use.

These days zero commissions have become a mainstay of the market. While this sounds great on the surface, there's a lot going on under the hood that you need to be aware of. The obvious question is, how does the broker make money if they don't charge you commissions? There are two business models that enable them to do so.

The first is implemented by the likes of large brokerage houses such as Charles Schwab and Fidelity. These brokerage houses are one-stop shops, and they offer a large number of financial products to their customers. You can trade for zero commissions but you'll also be pushed to sign up for wealth management products, IRAs and so on. This allows the broker to make money from service fees for those products.

They also make money by earning interest on your account deposits. This is why they'll insist on a large minimum balance. The more you deposit, the more they make off interest. This is a pretty transparent model.

The second business model is a bit more opaque and currently lies in a gray area in the United States. It is how Silicon Valley darlings such as Robinhood manage to survive. Here's how it works. The broker takes your order and passes it on to a market maker. Market makers are usually one of the large investment banks. They could be handled by a human being or an algorithm.

These days, it's usually an algorithm that is overseen by a human. Let's say you placed an order to buy 100 shares of a stock that was selling for $5 currently. The market maker looks at the market and buys as many shares as they can for this price. Let's say they accumulate 100 shares for $5.01.

They then turn around and sell you the stock for $5.02. In this trade, they've made a profit of $1. This doesn't sound like much at all. However, it's relatively risk-free, and they make millions of such trades every day. Imagine them making one million dollars' worth of trades every day and clearing one cent on every trade. That's $10,000 in profit every day.

Market makers trade tens, and even hundreds of millions worth of trades every day in the stock market. The profits that they make on these trades are split with the likes of Robinhood. That's how the broker makes money from your trades.

If you're a long-term investor, this isn't a bad thing for you. After all, given the potential capital gains appreciation over time, you'll not notice the loss of less than 0.2% per share. However, it's a different story for traders. Your entries are far more important and the smallest of price fluctuations can change your bottom line.

In effect, you're paying 0.2% as commissions to enter a trade. A broker that charges commissions usually charges less than 0.1% of your trade value as commissions. So who is the cheaper broker here?

There's another issue with the likes of such zero commission apps. The broker is placed in a massive conflict of interest with their client. They're not being paid for executing your trades efficiently. They're being paid on the basis of the price they sell you stocks.

Technically speaking, the market maker is another institution, and they're the ones selling you the stock. However, the broker is compensated from the sale. While this structure allows them to circumvent FINRA's rule on brokers not trading against their customers, it's a technicality that they're relying on.

The bottom line is, if you're a serious trader or want to be one, stay away from these apps and opt for brokers such as IB or TradeStation that charge you commissions. These brokers will get you the best price possible no matter what and will not inflate the price of the stock before selling it back to you.

Account Types

There are two types of accounts you can sign up for with a broker. The first is cash and the other is margin. A cash account allows you to only place long trades. There are two ways of placing trades in the market. Going long means you buy the stock first in the hopes of a price rise. Once its price rises, you sell it at the higher price and make a profit.

The other way is to go short. In this method, you sell the stock first and then hope that its price declines. Once it does decline, you buy it back for this lesser price and earn a profit.

Cash accounts don't allow you to go short. To do this you need a margin account. Margin in trading terms implies borrowing, either of cash or stock. In order to go short, you're selling something you don't own. Thus, your broker needs to borrow the stock you wish to short and you'll have to pay interest on this.

The good news about trading penny stocks is that you don't ever need to short a stock. After all, these stocks are already trading around $5 or so. How much lower can they go? The better play is to buy low and sell high, in that order; so going long is the best move.

Given that margin accounts require higher minimum balances, this is a very good thing. The downside of using a cash account to trade is that your trades will settle after two days. For example, if you sell something on Monday the cash from that sale will be credited to your account on Wednesday.

This means if you have a low account balance, you can't trade in the interim. A higher account balance will solve this issue but you might run into this hurdle at first. Another hurdle to watch out for is the Pattern Day Trader rule or PDT.

PDT is given to us by FINRA and aims to protect traders from themselves. A PDT is someone who places more than four trades over five consecutive days (*Pattern Day Trader*, 2020). Keep in mind that selling or exiting your position is also considered a trade. If you are classified as a PDT, you'll need to deposit at least $25,000 in your account to continue trading.

This is a huge hurdle for traders that don't have access to large amounts of capital. Most penny stock traders choose this asset class because they have low capital balances. So how can you navigate this? There are a few options available.

The first is to restrict your trading activity until you reach the $25,000 mark. This will take time and it can be frustrating for you to let go of good opportunities to avoid being hit with PDT. Some traders choose to hang onto their positions for far too long in order to escape the trade limits, but this is not a good way to trade.

The second option is to trade either the futures or the options of the stock. With regular stocks, this works a charm. Options and futures are derivative instruments that mimic the movement of the underlying stock. Both of them have monthly expirations and, as long as you stay away from the contracts that are expiring within a week, you can trade them successfully.

In the case of options, you must keep in mind that the price you pay for the option, called its premium, is an amount you will lose no matter what. Therefore, you need to take this hurdle into account when exiting your trade for a profit.

Options and futures traders don't have to worry about PDT because these instruments are regulated by another regulatory body. FINRA doesn't have purview over them and therefore you can trade them as much as you want.

However, the truth is that most penny stocks will have no options and futures or extremely low trading volumes in their contracts. As a result, you might find yourself operating in something that is effectively an OTC instrument. You should check the price spread to see if it mimics the spread of the underlying stock. If it doesn't, stay away from it.

Now that you're up to speed with regard to the regulations, let's take a look at the advantages and disadvantages of trading penny stocks.

Advantages

There's a lot to like about trading penny stocks and I've touched upon these briefly thus far. Let's take a look at them in more detail.

Big Winners

There are tons of great companies that trade for pennies. These companies are regularly the target of speculators and, given how low their prices are, any rise in them is spectacular in nature. For example, a stock that is trading for $1 only needs to rise by $1 to gain 100%.

This isn't far-fetched since all stocks trading above a dollar tend to move in fractions of 50 cents. This means a single tick, or price move will result in a 50% move in price. Stocks trading for a dollar regularly move up to many multiples of that, thereby netting their owners a huge gain.

Return on Time

As I mentioned earlier, penny stocks provide traders with a far better return on their time invested when compared to regular stocks. A stock that is priced at $100 needs to move by $50 to produce a 50% gain. It's going to move in increments of 50 cents, just like the penny stock will.

The work you need to put into analyzing the stock is exactly the same as with the penny stock. You need to look at the charts, look at the fundamentals and screen them using the same parameters. So why not trade the asset that appreciates a lot quicker and gives you a better return on your money?

Low Barrier of Entry

Penny stocks cost almost nothing. As a result, entering this market isn't going to create much of a burden on you in terms of capital requirements. If you have just $500 to trade, you can buy as many as 500 shares in a stock that's trading for a dollar. If you buy a stock trading for 50 cents, then you can own as many as 1,000 shares.

If the price moves by just one dollar, you stand to make either $500 or $1,000 in next to no time! Penny stocks tend to move a lot faster than their more pricey counterparts because a short distance tends to create huge gains. Rises of 100% or 200% are normal and this gives you a huge opportunity to make lots of money, quickly.

Disadvantages

There are downsides to trading penny stocks, just like there is everything else. You should read all of these to make sure they're suited for you before jumping in to trade them.

Not Always Reliable

While there are many companies trading for a dollar that are excellent, the vast majority of penny stocks are terrible and have no value attached to them. If you stick to Tier One and Tier Two stocks, you'll steer clear of outright frauds.

The OTC markets are a free for all and many investors fall prey to them. Those stocks tend to have attractive prices and move in large fractions. Imagine a stock selling for just one cent that moves in fractions of 10 cents. That's a 100% gain with just a single tick! The flip side is that a single tick can also mean a 100% loss.

Therefore, you need to be very careful when doing your homework on these stocks. Do not try to shortcut the process or try to get-rich-quick. You're trading to make lots of money quickly.

However, this is different from having a get-rich-quick mindset that seeks to shortcut the hard work you'll need to carry out to earn rewards.

The Odds are Against you

I mentioned in the introduction that 90% of traders lose their money within the first year of opening their accounts. This is because all of them fail to practice the principles of good trading. Happily, this disadvantage is straightforward to overcome. You need to follow a good framework for success and if you execute it well, you'll be successful.

This brings us back to the kind of mindset you're carrying. You cannot expect to become rich overnight. You'll read a lot about traders who turned $1,000 into a million and live in penthouses, etc. However, a lot of these people make money selling courses to other traders. In most cases, they don't trade their own money anymore.

The markets keep changing and, in order to stay on top of them, you have to devote a lot of time to analyzing them. Someone who's running a course and publishing YouTube videos about million dollar trades is probably not up to speed with how things are. Sure, they might be good resources for basic knowledge...but understand that you're going to have to put in a lot of work to be successful.

It's surprisingly easy to fail at trading. Make sure you stick to the path outlined in this book and you'll be successful. I can't promise you how long it's going to take. All I can say is that it'll be worth it once you get there.

Different Rules

I spent an entire section outlining the regulations, so what is this section about? Well, this comes from stockbrokers imposing their own conditions on trading penny stocks. Some brokers just don't want the business or will want customers with certain capital sizes to trade with them.

This means the broker will charge you money to trade penny stocks in order to discourage you from doing so. These costs will add up over time, so you should take the time to clarify whether you can trade penny stocks without incurring additional charges.

If a stock happens to be too thinly traded, the broker might prevent you from even buying it. This is why it pays to choose a large and highly reputed broker if you wish to trade penny stocks successfully.

Chapter 2:

Price Charts

The basis of any successful trading operation is the price chart. How well you can read it, and perform an analysis of it, will determine your overall success when it comes to trading. Price charts can be both simple and tough to read, all at once. Many traders find that they have an intuitive grasp of how to reach charts, but when the time comes to place trades on it, everything goes wrong.

The very first thing that confounds beginners is that prices are depicted very differently on trading charts. On CNBC, you'll simply see AMZN or any other company as selling for $2,500 or a single number. When you go ahead and try to trade AMZN, you'll find yourself hit with two prices.

These prices are the spread, and understanding this is crucial for your success. The spread consists of a buying price and a selling price. The buying price is called the ask and the selling price is called the bid. Another way to look at it is that the bid is always lower than the ask.

With regard to penny stocks, this is extremely important to know. If the stock moves in ticks of 50 cents, the spread will likely be a dollar or so apart. For example, you can sell the stock for $1 and buy it for $2. If the tick size is 10 cents, you can expect the spread to be a lot lower, but it will be higher than the tick size at the very least.

You should stick to trading stocks that have low spreads. This can be illustrated via an example. Let's say stock A has a spread of $1/$2 and B has a spread of $1/$1.20. If you bought A, you'll have paid a price of $2 to enter. Since you can only sell at the bid price, you need the bid to be equal to at least $2 to break even on your trade (before commissions and taxes).

That means you need the stock to move 100% in order to simply break even. If the stock's tick size is 50 cents, this is a reasonable expectation. After all, a 100% percent move is just two ticks. However, if the tick size is 10 cents, you'll likely never realize any gains on this stock. To simply break even, you need 10 ticks to move in your favor. While this might happen, it certainly increases your odds of failure.

Compare the tick size to the spread to get a feel of how likely the stock is to make you money. If there's too much of a gap between these numbers, you're best off staying away from it. Determining this is as easy as looking at the stock move on your trading software for a while before entering a position in it. See how often or how soon it covers the spread or crosses the spread. This will give you an idea of how likely it is for you to make any money on it.

On the flip side, choosing stocks that have low spreads and high tick sizes can backfire. If the tick size is equal to the spread, you'll need to take into account that an adverse movement can result in a quick loss. There is no standard tick size, or spread combination, I can give you (unfortunately).

Just make sure the spread is in proportion to the tick size and observe stocks before jumping into them. The framework I will provide you with in this book will ensure you do this successfully.

Now that you've understood the spread, it's time to tackle one of the biggest hurdles of them all: Price depiction.

Candlesticks

Financial news channels portray price in a manner that makes no sense to traders. You'll usually see a line that fluctuates up and down and some intelligent looking symbols placed around it. This is what price is, you'll be told. The truth is that these kinds of line charts are great when you want to sound intelligent.

However, when you want to make intelligent decisions, especially in trading, they're pretty much useless. A line chart can help summarize long-term market movements but, in the short-term, price is too dynamic to be able to be made sense of with such simple charts.

What you need is a sophisticated chart that gives you a lot of information in a single glance. A lot of traders in North America use a type of chart called the bar chart. These charts convey four important pieces of information to the trader: The open, high, low and close.

Price charts depict different time frames within them. For example, a daily chart shows how price behaved on a daily basis within that day's session. A 60-minute chart divides the market session into 60-minute intervals and the chart displays what happened within them.

Below the 60-minute is the 30-minute, 15 minute, five-minute and one minute. There's also the tick chart but this is almost never traded. The 30-minute chart divides each 60-minute interval into two 30-minute ones, the 15-minute divides the 30-minute into two and so on. A single 60-minute bar is divided into 60 individual price bars on the one-minute chart as a result.

Different traders operate on different timeframes. The choice of time frame depends on what suits you best. The time frame that gives traders a good mix of breathing room and feedback is the 60-minute chart.

New price bars are formed every 60 minutes on this chart so you'll need to check in once every hour. An hour also doesn't happen to be very long in the grand scheme of things and as a result, price moves fast enough for the trader to see some action, but not so fast that the trader feels overwhelmed.

Contrast this to the five-minute or one minute, where new bars are printed at those intervals.

While bars are useful, there's a much better way to represent price on charts. This is done by using candlesticks.

Basics

Figure 1 : Candlestick Chart

The chart in Figure 1 represents a daily timeframe. This means every bar or candle you see on it represents one entire day's worth of price action. On the bottom of this chart, towards the right-hand side I've highlighted the three different parts of a candlestick (also called bar).

The colored portion, which can be either black or white (or any other color combination) is called the body. The vertical line on top of the body is called the wick and the line sticking out below the body is called the tail. Together, all of these elements give the trader tons of information about the open, high, low and close.

The open is the price level at which the bar started. The high is the highest price level it hit during that interval, the low is the lowest level it went to and the close is where it finished the interval. Each interval is represented by a single bar here. This is a daily chart so every single bar represents a single market session.

If we were to dive below this time frame, we'd be at the 60-minute level. Here, every bar would represent an hour's worth of price action. The first place to begin our analysis of candlesticks is with the color of the bar's body. Throughout this book, I'll be using black and white as the two primary colors.

A candle that is colored black is a bearish candle. Bearish in a trading context means that price decreased. In contrast, bullish refers to situations where price increased. In other words, if you see a candle colored black in this book, it indicates that prices closed lower than the level they opened at.

The lowest point of a dark colored candle's body (not the tail, just the body) indicates the close. The highest point indicates the open.

In contrast, bars that are colored white are bullish in nature. This means prices increased over that interval. Therefore, the close is the highest point of the body and the open is the lowest point of the body.

The high of that interval is represented by the highest point of the wick while the low is represented by the lowest point of the tail. These two are the same whether the bar is bullish or bearish.

While candlesticks give us a clear view of how price behaved in an interval, their real power lies in painting a clear picture of the underlying order flow. What is meant by order flow? Quite simply, it's the sum of all the buy and sell orders that have been placed in that stock.

In Figure 1, we can see how prices move downwards and then jump back up. Notice how the size of the candle bodies on the left are tiny while they expand to huge proportions on the right. All of this is valuable information if you wish to trade successfully. The size of the candle bodies, the extent of their tails and wicks, and comparing them to previous candles, helps us understand how the bulls and bears are faring in the market.

If the market has an excess of bears over bulls, prices fall. Similarly, if bulls are greater in number, the markets will rise. The trick is to be able to spot those moments that indicate the balance of power is changing. Think of it as positioning yourself in front of a wave just as it's about to gather steam and come crashing down toward the short.

If you try to catch it too soon, you'll simply ride over it. If you're too late, the wave will come crashing down upon you and you'll have a pretty tricky time of it. Successful trading is all about getting the timing right. This is in opposition to long-term investing where time is not much of a factor at all.

The nature of candlesticks gives us information about this bullish to bearish balance. Whether markets move in a given direction or whether they move sideways, there are always indications provided by them. Candlesticks typically form patterns that help traders figure out the impending direction of price.

Let's take a look at some of these to see how order flow can be deciphered.

Patterns

All candlestick patterns are either continuation or reversal indicators. Some patterns function as both depending on the context in which price has behaved previously. Before getting into patterns I'd like to say that you should not think of these patterns as being infallible.

You'll understand this point a lot better when reading about risk management. For now, understand that successful trading is all about understanding probabilities. It isn't about being right every single time. You can be right 99% of the time and still lose money. You'll never be right 100%. Thus, it isn't about finding an infallible pattern.

It's about finding the pattern that's right more often than not and aligning yourself with what it says. The other thing to remember when it comes to candlesticks is that a single pattern by itself doesn't have the power to dictate order flow.

Instead, it is order flow that dictates the success of the pattern. What does this mean exactly? Let's say you spot a pattern that indicates a reversal of prices. However, if the prior price action doesn't indicate that one side of the market is weakening, and that the other is about to take over, the pattern doesn't mean anything.

Too many traders assume the opposite. They think that the mere presence of the pattern is enough to dictate order flow. This is not the case at all. The market doesn't care about fancy patterns. At the end of the day, supply and demand drive prices along with a healthy dose of emotion. A great pattern for one trader might be a terrible one for another.

When studying all of these patterns, keep in mind that you need prior conditions to be in place. Otherwise, the pattern isn't a valid one.

Three Line Strike

This is a bullish reversal pattern. In other words, it indicates that a bearish move is about to come to a close and that a bullish move is about to begin. As with all candlestick patterns, the best way to understand this pattern is to understand the order flow mechanics behind it, instead of memorizing its geometrical shape.

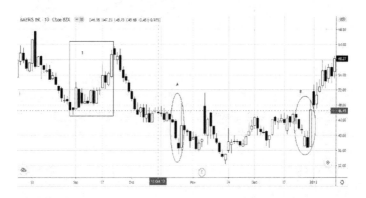

Figure 2 : Three Line Strike

Figure 2 indicates two three-line strike patterns at A and B. Neither of these are perfect patterns and this is on purpose. Geometrically speaking, the three-line strike looks a lot like the shape at A. Instead of having a bullish bar with a long wick, the bullish bar's body is strong with little to no wick. The pattern consists of four bars with the first three being bearish and the final one being a large bullish bar that engulfs the ones that came before it.

If you were to search for a perfect shape such as the one just described, odds are good that you'll keep searching for the rest of your life. Candlesticks have been around for centuries now (since the 1600s to be precise) and it stands to reason that all the patterns they exhibit have been deciphered by traders everywhere.

In order to succeed at using them, you need to understand why they work. This means understanding the order flow. Think of your task as finding the spirit behind the pattern instead of the precise shape. More often than not these days, a pattern that looks perfect leads to a loss.

What are the order flow characteristics of this pattern? Simply put, it indicates weakening bearish strength and overwhelming bullish strength. This is why the final bullish bar overcomes everything else that preceded it. Behind the scenes, the bulls are overcoming the bears and are exerting their strength.

It stands to reason that this sort of overwhelming bullishness cannot express itself unless the bears have already been weakening. What I mean is that if the bears are truly strong, no amount of bullishness is going to overcome them. Any indication of strong bullishness is probably a case of the bears allowing the bulls temporary respite, as opposed to it being a true show of bullish strength.

This is why the box marked with the number '1' is so important. Notice that prior to this pattern forming, the bulls pushed back into the bearish trend. Notice that the angle of the bullish move is almost equal to that of the bearish move. Angles and the size of price bars are great indicators of the distribution of strength in the markets.

In this case, the size of the bars don't provide much of a clue but the angle does. When you're spotting the three-line strike pattern, look for such evidence of counter trend strength. Countertrend refers to the direction that is opposite the existing trend. In this case the counter trend is bullish.

Having established that the bears are weakening, we arrive at the first pattern labeled A. This is pretty close to a perfect three-line strike. It has the three bearish bars descending in order and a huge bullish bar. Sure, it isn't perfect, but what is? The novice trader will either stay away from this thinking it isn't perfect or will jump in thinking that it's close to perfect and that close is good enough.

They'll neglect to give value to the large wick on the bullish bar. That wick indicates that the bulls pushed prices up but the bears pushed them right back down. What's more, the bars did this when the bulls were strong.

This means while the bears are losing strength, they're not fully done just yet. I'm not saying that every single wick on a strong bullish bar means this. The conclusion drawn here depends on the price action that preceded it. With this background in place, the right move is to ignore this pattern.

Moving ahead, we see price fall lower which validates what we concluded about bearish strength. However, notice that after the fall, there are almost no bearish bars present. Almost every bar is bullish. This indicates that the bears have probably been overcome for good. Any reversal signal that prints now has a high probability of success.

Such a signal occurs at B. Notice that this pattern isn't a three-line strike at first glance. All it has is a huge engulfing bullish bar. The bars before it aren't particularly bearish as the geometry dictates it ought to be.

Notice that while the shape is off, the order flow conforms to what the three-line strike indicates. Weak bearish pressure being overcome by strong bullish price action. This bullishness is so strong that it engulfs the entire range of price action that preceded it. This is a perfectly valid three-line strike despite containing six lines within it and despite having a bullish bar within the bearish portion of the pattern.

This is how you need to trade price patterns. Don't search for pretty shapes. Understand what the order flow indicates and look for indications that the pattern will succeed. This is done by looking for clues before the pattern even prints.

To trade this pattern, buy on the close of the engulfing bar and place your stop loss order below the low of this bar. The stop loss order protects your downside. If the market falls below that price, your position is liquidated.

You might be wondering what your position size ought to be? In other words, how many shares should you buy? I'll cover this in detail in the risk management chapter.

Two Black Gaps

Figure 3: Two Black Gaps

This is a bearish continuation pattern. As the name suggests, it's composed of two bearish bars, one after another, with a gap in between them. A gap occurs in the market when the close of one bar doesn't line up with the open of another. Gaps in the stock market usually occur when the market opens the next day.

Overnight supply and demand means that the levels at which price opens the next day are not the same as the ones at which they closed the previous day. Figure 3 illustrates such a pattern as well as what a gap looks like. Some traders look for clean gaps. In other words, they look for gaps that are not covered by the second candle's wick.

The gap shown here isn't a clean one but once again, it's best for you to focus on the underlying order flow instead of worrying about the geometry of the pattern. The two black gaps pattern indicates a massive buildup of bearish pressure. This pressure is so large that prices fall massively, thereby creating the gap.

A bearish gap of this sort cannot be created without the complete absence of bulls. If you think about it, prices manage to go lower only because there's someone willing to buy the stock at those lower prices. In the absence of bulls, bears won't have anyone else to trade with and this causes them to go even lower in order to find them.

Consequently, you want to look for this pattern after it has become evident that the bulls have all but vanished from the market. The best place to find it is right after the end of a long bull trend. While the two black gap patterns won't help you pinpoint the exact end of the bull trend, it will help you enter the bearish trend pretty early.

At the very least, you want the size of both bars to be big in comparison to the previous bullish bars. Remember to look for the signs of a bull trend coming to an end. This can include the increased presence of bears and the lack of bullish movement. Looking for the presence of lower highs is also a good move since these indicate that the bulls are disappearing.

Enter on the close of the second bar and place your stop above the gap.

While it isn't an official pattern, the bullish variation of this would have two bullish bars one after another with a gap in between them. This is because if you apply the same order flow principles to a bullish scenario, we arrive at the same conclusion.

Hammer

The hammer is a bullish pattern that works as both a continuation and a reversal pattern. Figure 4 illustrates this.

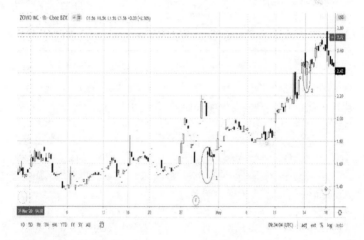

Figure 4: Hammer

There are two hammers indicated in Figure 4 and both of them are valid signals. The hammer is a bar, bullish or bearish, that has a small body with a large tail. The tail indicates that bears tried pushing prices down but were repulsed by the bulls.

When looking for a bullish reversal, you want to see whether there's been enough evidence that the bears are losing strength. After all, in order for a bullish reversal to take place, the bears have to exit the market. Without this, a hammer is worthless.

Figure 4 also illustrates one of the challenges of trading penny stocks. Notice how ZVO (the stock in question) prints many gaps and bars where no trades take place. This often happens with stocks that have high spreads and low tick sizes. Traders are simply not interested in the stock and as a result, price jumps around.

It is still possible to trade these stocks but you'll have to remain in the position for a lot longer than usual. In this case, if you took the first hammer at 1 you would have netted a huge gain of almost 50%. The second hammer results in a similar gain down the road. The downside is that you would have had to hold on to these positions for almost three days to realize these gains.

Throughout that time you would have had to deal with there being zero activity in the stock and the constant risk of it gapping past your stop loss level. This is referred to as slippage. When the market jumps past your stop loss level, your broker will execute the order at whichever price is prevalent in the market. If the prevailing prices happen to be three or four points below where you wished to exit, that is the price you'll get.

Slippage is a huge risk since it adds to your losses considerably. There's nothing you can do about it either. All you can do is avoid stocks like the one in Figure 4 and stick to highly traded ones.

Hammers are also best utilized near areas of support. Let's look at what this means exactly.

Chapter 3:

Support and Resistance

Support and resistance analysis cuts right to the heart of technical analysis. These are important zones on the price chart where traders interact with one another or wait for the right price to hit. Support and resistance zones (sr) are also where traders emphasize their beliefs about a market and the direction it ought to take.

If you've even glanced at a trading chart previously, you might have noticed a large number of horizontal lines drawn across it. This is how sr is identified on a chart. Despite a single line being drawn, they tend to be zones. How are these zones formed and why are they so important for trading successfully?

An sr zone originally forms thanks to some important event taking place. The exact nature of this event is immaterial. What matters is that buyers or sellers decided to make a stand at this point and push prices back the other way. You've already seen how order flow is produced, thanks to bulls and bears in the market interacting with one another.

An sr zone is where there is a preponderance of either bulls or bears. A zone that has a large number of bears will usually result in a resistance zone. This is where prices will be pushed down from. Conversely, a zone that has a large number of bulls will result in a support zone, where prices will be propped up from.

Given that you'll be focused almost exclusively on placing long trades, you might think that support zones are all you need to focus on. This is incorrect. Analyzing and identifying resistance zones is important if you want to exit your trades at the right profit levels and to evaluate whether your trade has a chance of working out or not.

For example, you might enter long at a level but if there's a huge resistance level looming ahead, the chances of it working out are low. The best place to begin with sr analysis is to identify the characteristics of important sr zones.

Swing Points

Swing points refer to points on the chart where price switches direction. For example, if it's been moving down for a while and then swing upwards, a swing low has just been created. If it moves upwards and then swings down, a swing high has been created.

These points form great sr zones since they're a pretty clear indication of where the bulls and bears have positioned themselves in the market. From a trader's perspective, they're easy to analyze because the process is quite visual. Here are the things you need to look at in order to figure out how strong a swing point is:

- The angle with which price arrives at the point, and the angle with which it leaves
- The extent and strength of the bars that leave the point

Angles

Angles are a very important element of sr analysis. A steep angle indicates a lot of momentum and strength with very little counter trend opposition. A shallow one indicates a lack of strength. If a level can hold off a strong attack, it's a signal that the counter trend traders at that level are pretty strong.

The angle of attack by itself isn't an indicator. You need to compare it to the angle with which price leaves the level too. Often what happens is that price may attack an sr level at a steep angle but the counter trend traders will only be able to push prices weakly off that level.

While they were strong enough to hold the level they weren't strong enough to push prices back the other way. You want both elements to be in place. Price leaving at a shallow angle is a good indication of strength.

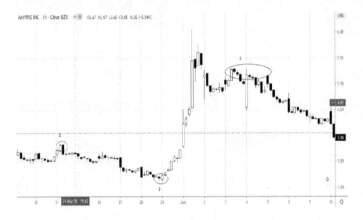

Figure 5: Swing Points

Figure 5 illustrates three examples of what swing points are and what they aren't. First off, I'd like to point out that the circle indicated by the number 3 is an example of what a swing point isn't. While price does reach this level and then swings down, notice that this isn't a single point as much as it is an extended level where price bars cluster.

You want the footprint on a swing point to be as small as possible. Towards the left of the chart, we have two examples labeled 1 and 2. 1 is an example of a swing point that is a weak resistance level. The bulls push strongly into it.

Notice the consecutive bars that led into the level and the angle of attack. The bears mustered one strong bearish bar in response but then notice how price drifts downward instead of moving purposefully. The extent to which price moves down is greater but notice the angle is a lot shallower than the angle with which the bulls attacked the level.

This indicates that the bears at this level are weak. Is it any wonder that once prices reach the same level further down the road, it barely pauses at it?

This upswing is produced from swing point 2. This is a textbook example of a strong swing point. Notice the angle of attack versus the angle with which price leaves the point. Notice how strongly price leaves and how it seemingly gains bullish momentum from it.

Once prices come back down to this level, if it ever does, this level will act as a strong support zone. The bulls will take note of how well it was defended previously and every trader in the market will flock to this zone in the hopes of it being defended. Whether the level will hold or not is impossible to tell. But that's not the point.

The important thing to note is that the level has a high probability of holding once price comes back down to it.

Horizontal Zones

Figure 5 spotlighted a place on the chart labeled 3 that was not a swing point. Despite this not being a swing point, it is an example of another type of sr zone. These zones are ones that price repeatedly tests before swinging in the opposite direction. Take another look at figure 5 and notice how the level extends to the left of the circle as well where the gap is.

A gap by itself isn't a great sr zone. However, if you notice prices retesting the gap or trying to fill it down the road and failing to go past it, it's a pretty good indication that the level is well defended. In this case, it's a strong resistance level.

These kinds of horizontal zones tend to act as good sr because price repeatedly tests them. The greater the number of times price tests a level, the stronger the zone is. Another thing to watch for is the gap between retests.

A longer gap (in terms of time) indicates strength. This is because if prices are pushed far away from the zone when the level is first tested, then it's going to take longer for them to come back to that level. A level that holds for long tends to perpetuate itself since the longer it holds, the more significance it gains and more traders flock to it.

A good example of this is from Figure 5, at the point labeled 2. This is a swing point when you look just at figure 5. However, scroll to the right and you'll see that there's more going on here. While it's still a swing point, a reason the bullish reaction was so strong was that it's part of a zone that was tested earlier and held.

Figure 6 illustrates this.

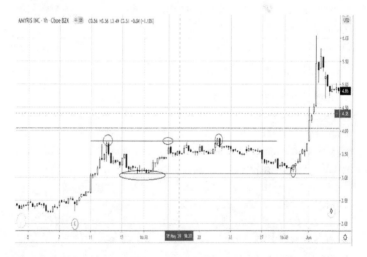

Figure 6: SR Levels

The swing point in question is indicated by the circle on the right-hand side of the chart. Notice to the left the repeated tests that this level underwent. While the tests weren't strong, notice how long it took for the bears to bring prices back to that level.

In contrast, notice how often the bulls pushed prices up to the resistance zone on top. After the initial test on the bottom, prices swing upwards and hover near there before swinging down. That swing down was point 1 labeled in Figure 5 as an example of a weak swing point.

Notice that the gaps between retests are small. This indicates that prices are not being pushed very far away from the level and are returning quickly. This is visually evident in Figure 6. The initial test of support that takes place is tricky to figure out and this tends to trip up a lot of traders.

Notice how prices bounce upwards and then come right back down and stay close to the level. The only indication of bullish strength we get from the level is when price finally leaves it. As such, until this occurs we would have labeled this as a weak level. However, the bulls step in at some point and prices rise higher.

These kinds of things happen in the market and you have no control over them. Prices will move when they want to. All you can do is read the odds. In this case, positioning yourself for a bullish entry anticipating the first retest would not have been a wise move. This is because there is no prior evidence that the bulls will support this level.

However, positioning yourself for a bullish entry at point 1 (to the right-hand side of the chart) is a smart move. Prices tested this level and the resistance above is weak. Therefore, it makes sense to anticipate a bullish push from here. Apparently, the majority of the market thought the same given the strength with which prices rocketed off the level.

Also notice that prices don't line up exactly in a straight line. This reinforces my point about them being zones and not horizontal levels. Most traders call them levels but successful traders understand that they're zones.

Broken Zones

Often what happens is that prices break past a level and then use the other side of that level to move further. In other words, if a resistance level is broken, prices retest the broken levels and use it as support to propel themselves higher. Often, strong sr levels behave in this way.

This happens because traders that defend the level turn to the other side of the market and join the path of least resistance.

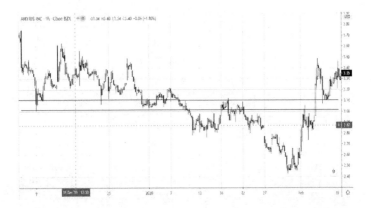

Figure 7: Changing Roles

Figure 7 illustrates a zone that acts as both support and resistance over a long period of time. Notice that on the left of the chart price repeatedly retests the level and it holds before breaking. Price then uses it as resistance before dipping downwards. It retests it as resistance once more before breaking above it and using it as support.

This particular zone is a wide one and needs two lines to mark its extent. This wide extent means it's tricky to trade but not impossible. Looking for valid signals in this zone would have produced a good number of profitable trades. Alternatively, you could have simply entered once prices reached the level, and then gone long off of it.

This method of trading might seem dangerous or unnatural to you. Yet, it is how many professional traders place their orders in the market. Very few professionals wait around for the market to throw them a signal before entering. You can use price action patterns as a signal, but relying on them entirely in the long run isn't a good move.

Instead, it's best to intelligently screen the appropriate stocks and to then look at the relevant sr levels present in them. Once you've identified the levels, you can place trades right off them in anticipation of a reaction from prices. This way, you'll open yourself up to both sides of the market and to more trade opportunities.

After all, not every trade opportunity prints as a price pattern. Remember that order flow is what creates these patterns in the first place. As long as you focus on the direction of order flow, you'll be able to enter the market in a profitable manner.

So how do you screen penny stocks properly? There are many such stocks in the market. How can you narrow them down properly to identify the ones you can take advantage of?

Chapter 4:

Screening Strategy

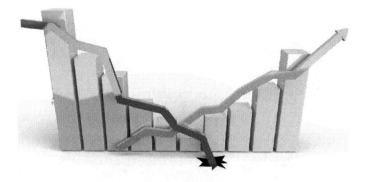

A huge part of your success when it comes to trading penny stocks is determined by how well you screen them. The stock market contains a large number of penny stocks that move for a variety of reasons. If you can screen the best opportunities, you'll be placing yourself in a much better position to take advantage of market conditions.

There are two ways of screening penny stocks: fundamental and technical. While some traders are pretty passionate about separating both of these into separate categories, it's best if you view them as being two types of tools that are often used together. For example, if you wish to hang a picture on the wall, you'll need a hammer and a screwdriver more often than not.

Trying to argue that one is better than the other is fruitless. Instead, your aim should be to use whichever method suits you best. Don't be afraid of combining both screening methodologies. You'll simply unearth better opportunities by doing this.

Let's begin by looking at fundamental screening methods.

Fundamentals

The fundamentals of a stock refer to the company's business. How well is it doing in terms of profits and revenues and how good are its operating margins? Is the business sector it's operating in lucrative or does it face headwinds? These are questions that long-term investors ask themselves before investing in a company.

Your task as a trader is to identify some of these aspects but not get bogged down with it. Remember that your time horizon is a lot smaller than that of an investor. You're looking for a stock that is going to move and move fast. This is what gives you the best return on your investment and time.

When screening for penny stocks, be it through fundamental or technical methods, your job is to unearth momentum. Momentum is a word that is bandied about quite a lot by many market experts but finding true momentum is tough. Usually, you need to use a combination of screens to find that quality stock.

When you do find it, you'll be rewarded amply. As you read through all of these screening methods, keep the point about momentum in mind. This is what we're after at the end of the day.

All of these screens can be set up through your broker's software or through special stock screening software. I'll list the best penny stock screening software at the end of this chapter.

Gaps

You've already learned about gaps and why they're caused. It should be obvious that a stock that gaps at the open is experiencing huge demand (if it has gapped up) and that this demand will likely push its prices even higher. You will need to discern the differences between low quality and high-quality gaps.

The quality of a gap can be determined in two ways. The first is to look at the size of the gap. If a stock opens five percent above its previous close, that is an enormous gap. In the case of penny stocks, the numerical amount of this gap might be low, but remember that the price of the stock is low to begin with. Focus on setting up a screen that monitors for large gap percentages, not amounts.

So what is a good gap percentage? Like with everything else in trading, it's tough to put a number on this. Some traders look for five percent while some look for three percent. It comes down to how comfortable you are with trading momentum. Stocks that gap up massively attract a lot of attention and you'll find their prices jump around quite a lot.

Combine this with the fact that the market open usually produces a ton of trading volumes and you'll see that price spreads will move quite a lot. Some traders are happier dealing with environments that aren't as sensitive. They prefer middle of the road gap percentages that are more in line with the pace at which they can trade well.

The best time to run this screen is right after the market opens. Most penny stocks traders will find that the first hour after the market opens is where 90% of their money will be made. Attention is high during this time and everyone is scrambling to get into the market. Overnight orders are being executed in a rush and as a result, prices move quickly.

Of course, gaps do occur during other times as well. They mostly occur around earnings announcements or other special events. I'll cover these shortly since they're screens by themselves.

For now, understand that gaps indicate serious movement potential. There is some danger of gaps being overextended. A stock that gaps up too much will attract bears and you'll find that the price will decline. How do you spot such stocks? For starters, look for the presence of overhead resistance. The stronger it is, the more likely a fall is.

You can wait for prices to move past that resistance level or wait to buy at a lower support level. I'll also be showing you a technical analysis strategy that you can use to determine the strength of selling in the market.

The best way to figure out your preference of gaps is to paper trade for a while before going live. I'll be providing you with a great paper trading framework towards the end of this book that will allow you to execute your strategies in a low-risk environment before risking real money.

Percentage Gainers

Closely related to gaps are percentage earners. Often demand comes in after the market has opened as opposed to overnight. This causes a stock to open roughly at the same level as the previous close and then shoot up in price. The best way to track such stocks is to run a high percentage gainer screen.

This will give you the list of stocks that have gained the most when compared to their previous closing prices. You will end up screening in a lot of gapping stocks through this so you can combine the two methods with one another.

Keep in mind that a high percentage gain along doesn't mean the stock is going to keep rising. A good example of this is a stock that gaps up too much and then starts to go sideways or decline in an effort to cover the gap. This stock will still show up as a high percentage gainer but its true nature in that moment is bearish.

You'll have to sift through and find the stocks that are truly behaving in a bullish manner. I say bullish because with penny stocks it's far more profitable to go long than short. Focus mostly on bullish opportunities and you'll see your money growing a lot faster.

The best way of quickly determining whether a large percentage gainer is worth your time is to take a look at the sr levels close by. If it manages to breach a good resistance level, then you can use that broken level as support to get in on the uptrend. You can also take a look at the news and see whether such a high rise in prices is justified or not.

New Weekly High

Hopefully, you're sensing a pattern by this point. Our aim is to find the stocks that are moving up and fast. The new weekly high screen is a great one because a lot of traders focus on weekly parameters when it comes to finding great stocks. This is because most traders hang onto their positions for close to a week.

As a result, a stock that is peeing out above its previous weekly high is an excellent candidate to attract the attention of other traders in the market. The new high could have been driven by some news item or some other special situation. It really doesn't matter from a trading perspective.

All you need to realize is that momentum is with this stock and you need to get in on it as quickly as you can at a sensible level. While the screen is a potent one, most traders use it incorrectly. They tend to jump in the minute prices rise to new highs. This is a poor way of trading.

Instead, you need to wait for it to provide you with an opportunity at a good sr level. If it's just broken out past a strong resistance level, then you can enter immediately. However, if it's in between levels, wait for it to reach some support level that can provide you with a good entry.

This is a great example of how you should blend fundamental and technical factors together to generate trade opportunities.

News Watch

These days, many trading firms have developed algorithms that scan Twitter and news feeds for mention of companies and other stock names. These algorithms range from sophisticated to rudimentary keyword searches but it highlights the importance of following the news as a trader.

Most traders cannot spend time building an algorithm and testing it. Besides, by doing this you're only going to pit yourself against the big players who have unlimited amounts of capital. Instead of playing a game you can't win, focus on gaining an advantage through other ways.

This is a slower screen than the other ones mentioned here. You'll need to conduct your research during off market hours and scan the news for mentions of things such as lawsuits, settlements and other interesting items. The announcement of an investment from a large institution or a merger is something else that should be on your radar.

While all of these count as special situations, your aim here is to watch for follow-up news items during the trading session. For example, if you're familiar with a company's fortunes through prior research and then see a news item declaring that the company has a brand-new product tied to some market need, you'll be in a good position to jump in on the price rise immediately.

Truth be told, this is an unsustainable way of trading over the long run. However, every now and then you're going to unearth great opportunities that will give you huge returns. It's also an open-ended screen. In fact, think of it as being market research instead of a screen.

The more you familiarize yourself with the stocks and markets you're operating in, the more lucrative this method will prove itself to be.

Low Float

Float refers to the number of outstanding shares a company has in the market that is available for trading. Many penny stock companies have large amounts of float because they need to raise as much capital as they can. Remember that most of these companies are unprofitable and aren't run well.

Issuing stock is an easy way for them to raise more money to finance their business. The problem is that when a large amount of stock is issued, this dilutes the ownership of existing stockholders. As a result, prices move a lot slower. The market also tends to ignore such companies since the odds of them being well run are close to none.

The net result is that it takes a lot of effort and events of significant magnitude for such companies to rise to higher price levels. Instead, focus on low float companies. These companies are well run and due to a small number of shares being present, they tend to be in higher demand.

Typically, companies that have float levels of less than 20% are considered excellent candidates. The way to calculate float is to look at a company's balance sheet and find the number of issued shares. This will be noted in the 'Shareholder's equity' section at the bottom.

Now subtract the number of restricted shares and preferred shares (also noted in the balance sheet) and you'll arrive at the float number.

Technical Screens

These screens depend on a variety of technical analysis factors and indicators. I'll dive deeper into indicators in the next chapter. For now, keep these in mind and look for ways to combine them with the fundamental screens you've just learned about.

200 EMA Crossover

To understand this better, we need to take a step back and understand what an exponential moving average or EMA is. The EMA is a technical analysis indicator that is plotted as a line or a curve over the price bars. This is a moving average of the previous n bars on the chart, where n is user defined.

For example, the 20 EMA is a curve that plots the average closing price of the previous 20 price bars. The 10 EMA is that of the previous 10 bars and so on. An EMA with a lower 'n' value is more sensitive to price changes. After all, it's measuring a small number of bears and will therefore pick up the slightest of price changes.

These EMAs are also called fast thanks to the speed with which they track these changes. In contrast, slow EMAs take a while to react to price changes. A popular trading system is the EMA crossover which I'll detail in the next chapter. There is another kind of crossover that traders monitor for.

This is the crossover between price and the 200 EMA. The 200 EMA is the 200 period moving average. If you're on the hourly chart, then the curve plots the average closing price of the last 200 hours, on the daily chart it's 200 days and so on. Many traders consider the 200 EMA to be an indicator of the line between bullishness and bearishness.

This is a belief that has long existed in the market. Some traders use it to figure out whether a stock is bullish or bearish. If it's above the 200 EMA they buy and if it's below the 200 EMA they sell. Of course, an actual trading system is more sophisticated than this but this is the basic way in which it works.

Instead of using the 200 EMA as a strategy, use it as a screen. If you spot prices crossing the 200 EMA from below (to above it) you can bet that many traders in the market will view this as a sign of bullishness. This means you can use the 200 EMA as support and enter with a stop below it.

The 200 EMA is an example of what is called dynamic resistance. The sr you learned about in the previous chapter are static. They don't move or change levels. The 200 EMA though moves and changes based on the past 200 price moves. This makes it dynamic.

It also serves as great support thanks to the belief that it indicates bullishness. Use it as such and you'll manage to get in on some great bullish moves. A better screen might be to look for prices that are approaching the 200 EMA from below. Watch for potential breakouts above this resistance and get in on the breakout.

Volume Spike

One of the great advantages of trading stocks over assets such as FX is that traders have complete access to volumes. Volumes indicate what other traders are doing in the market and, as a result, it becomes easy for you to decipher the veracity of certain moves. If you see a stock moving upwards, but on low volumes, this means the bears are likely to strike against it shortly.

This kind of trading is an example of using VSA or volume spread analysis to make trading entry decisions. It works only in the stock market or in markets that have reliable volume numbers. I'll cover this technique in the next chapter.

A volume spike is a great screen because it alerts you to two very important themes or types of trading in the market. The first type is exhaustion. Exhaustion refers to when a trend has ended. The traders who are pushing the trend forward expend a lot of effort to push prices and exhaust themselves by doing so. This allows the counter trend traders a good opportunity to enter the market and assert themselves.

As a result, prices move the other way very quickly and forcefully. Exhaustions usually occur within the market day and don't take place at the open or close. Look for bearish exhaustions to take advantage of the bull move in the other direction. It might not last long, but you can bet that it will be forceful and you can make a lot of money in a short period of time.

The other indication that a volume spike provides is increased demand. What you're looking for in both cases is a spike, not a mere increase. You want volumes to be at least greater than 10% of the average volumes over the preceding 10 bars. You can adjust these numbers and this will result in more sure short opportunities being screened in.

However, these will be far lesser in number. You want to find a sweet-spot between screening in enough opportunities and having them be good enough opportunities. When screening, most traders tend to make the mistake of trying to find 100% guaranteed wins.

It doesn't work this way. It's far better to screen in a lot of high probability opportunities and trade the ones that make the most sense to you. Instead of trying to hit home runs on every single trade, try to capture as many gains as you can. Your profit will take care of itself by doing this.

EMA Crossovers

I've already mentioned the price and EMA crossover screen. With this screen, which is also a strategy, you can monitor for fast EMAs crossing slow ones. A popular screen is to monitor the 5 EMA crossing the 20 EMA from below. This means the stock's previous five bars are showing bullishness that is above the average.

Some traders find this screen extremely sensitive and choose periods of 10 and 30 for the slow and fast EMAs respectively. Play around with these numbers when you paper trade. Keep in mind that certain stocks will respond better to different numbers. Again, use this screen as a general one that alerts you to good opportunities that you can dig into further.

All of these screens put together will provide you with a large list of potential stock ideas. In fact, you might need to trim this list down thanks to the number of opportunities you'll be screening in. At the very least, screening for low float stocks is a great idea and this should be your default screen no matter what.

A good way of using these screens is to build a large framework where these screens are progressive. For example, you first screen for low float stocks, then for volume spikes and then look for ones that are among the top in percentage gains for that session.

This will alert you to the best opportunities available. The key is to mix and match these screens and use them based on what you're comfortable with. Not every parameter or screen type will suit you and this is why experimenting in a low-risk environment through paper trading is so important.

The Best Screeners

If your broker's software terminal doesn't give you the ability to create screens of your own, you can use one of the software programs below. These are a mix of free and paid screeners. Don't hesitate to invest in a good penny stock screener since you'll more than make this money back when you realize a trading profit.

- Yahoo! finance
- FinViz
- MarketWatch
- Morningstar
- DojiSpace
- PastStat
- StockstoTrade

Chapter 5:

Fundamental Analysis

You've screened in some great stocks but how do you go about determining whether they're good enough to trade or not? Much like with screens, there are two ways for you to go about doing this. You can analyze the stocks' fundamentals or you can stick to looking at just the technicals.

Alternatively, you can combine the two approaches. The markets allow for a wide variety of approaches to be used in them and you should utilize the ones that make the most sense to you.

This chapter is going to cover all of the basic fundamental factors you can look at to determine how much a stock is likely to move and how far. Understand that the analysis I'll be detailing in this chapter is very different from the sort of analysis a long-term investor would carry out. Your objective is to simply figure out how likely the stock is to move in the short-term.

The long-term investor's objective is very different and their analysis is far more in-depth. From a trading perspective, fundamental analysis serves as a sanity check. As long as there are no gaping holes in the company's financial prospects, it's safe to trade it.

There are different resources you can use to analyze a company's fundamentals. The best resource is to use its 10-K filing. The 10-K is an annual report that every public company files with the SEC at the end of its fiscal year. This report details everything that is going on with the company's business and its outlook.

It's also written in a very specific tone of language that aims to reduce the marketing factor inherent in all company communications. This makes it a great resource to learn all about a company's business. The flip side is that these documents are long and require accounting knowledge.

You don't have to be an accounting expert but you do need to understand certain terms and jargon. Also, it takes time to go through them. Time is something you don't have as a trader. So what should you do?

Your objective should be to quickly look at the company's financial ratios and make sure they check out. Penny stocks can make you a lot of money but if you end up trading bad ones you'll have a lot of headaches to deal with. This is even if you stick to the ones that are traded on reputed exchanges. Financial ratio analysis is a good way to quickly determine what's going on with a company.

There are many different financial ratios that a company has. These involve all sorts of things such as cash flow, earnings, assets and so on. There are a few specific ratios that help you uncover the basic facts about a company. Using these will help you quickly analyze a company's prospects and figure out where you should trade it.

Earnings

Companies trade for low stock prices for a reason. They're not very profitable. More often than not, you'll find that penny stock companies don't even earn a profit. In some cases, they don't even have revenues!

Needless to say, you want the companies you're operating in to produce some sort of money. While the lack of a profit is not a bad thing by itself, you want to stick to companies that have shown the ability to make some sort of a profit in the past. This way you'll avoid a lot of the up and down movements that chronically unprofitable companies exhibit.

As for revenues, you definitely want them to be there. A lack of revenues will send the stock price tumbling quicker than you can imagine, and delisting will soon follow. This is a scenario you want to avoid at all costs.

Price to Earnings

The price to earnings or PE ratio is a metric that is used extensively in the markets. This is a ratio between the stock price and the earnings. A value that is non-existent indicates that the company isn't earning a profit. PE ratios cannot be negative and this is why any earnings below zero (a loss) simply results in a value of 'NA' being noted next to the stock.

Ratios that are extremely high tend to indicate overvalued stocks. Each sector has its own band of PE values that are appropriate. For example, technology stocks tend to attract high PE ratios since it's somehow okay for tech companies to burn through cash and make no money. Tesla is a good example of such a company. It makes cars but is somehow valued as a tech company and as a result, its stock is enormously overpriced.

However, it isn't a penny stock by any means, so I'm not going to spend time on it. A high PE ratio stock is something you should stay away from. High in this sense means high relative to the rest of the companies in its sector, not high in an absolute sense.

A PE of 50 might seem high to you but if the remaining companies in that sector are selling for a PE of 70, then 50 is a low number. High PE companies are terribly overvalued and have just one direction in which they can possibly go - down. This doesn't mean they'll decline immediately.

Betting on long using fundamentals is much better than using them to bet on shorts. This is because the average market participant doesn't like shorting and as a result, you'll find that even the most terrible of companies will take a long time to decline in value, no matter how justified the case is to short them.

When it comes to penny stocks you're looking at prices that aren't very high to begin with. In order to profit from a short, you want a high price since this gives you a lot of room to make money and exit. When a company's stock price declines by a large amount, management usually steps in with some announcement that stabilizes the stock.

This further reduces the cushion you have to make a profit. Add to this the fact that penny stocks are less liquid (have less traders in them) than average stocks and you have a situation where shorting is just not a sensible option. It won't offer you a good return on your time spent analyzing the stock.

Look for PE ratios to be on the lower end of the scale when searching for longs. This gives you the chance to capture both price appreciation as well as PE appreciation. The latter brings massive gains. For example, if a company is earning $1 per share and is selling for a PE of 10, its stock price is $10.

Let's say the PE grows to 30 and earnings remain the same. You've just netted a 200% gain (thanks to the stock price now being $30) and can also capture any gains that are brought about by earnings increasing. These two factors will power massive growth in the value of your stock.

Take the time to analyze the sector PE values when looking at stocks. Your broker, or even free screening resources such as Yahoo, will list this number along with the number for the company's competitors on the stock information page.

Price to Sales

You want companies that have some degree of revenues as I mentioned previously. The price to sales or PS ratio measures this. Since revenues will always be greater than profits, you'll see lower PS values than PE. Like with the PE, there is no definitive numerical scale that can be used.

Instead, a relative one is used wherein the trader or investor compares the PS value to others in the sector. You want to see values that are in line or close to the average. However, below average values are also acceptable. As long as the PE criteria is being met, you'll notice that the PS takes care of itself.

Like with the PE, you don't want to see an 'n/a' value here. This indicates that the company is either going out of business or is so incompetent that it can't generate even a single sale.

Needless to say you should stay away from such companies.

Price to Cash Flow

Earnings and cash flow are two different things. Earnings are an accounting creation. Cash flow is what comes into the bank. Most investors look at free cash flow when analyzing a company. Free cash flow refers to the amount of cash a company has after all expenses are paid for.

Not all expenses are deducted from income. For example, reinvestment into property and factories (called capital expenditures) are not deducted from earnings. The reason is that these expenses are necessary to maintain the competitive edge a company has. They're going back into assets that produce money and as a result, it doesn't make sense to subtract them.

However, a company cannot be competitive without this expense and needs to make enough cash to fund such investment. Thus, it also makes sense to subtract this value. This is why GAAP separates cash flow from earnings to provide investors with a better picture of how money is flowing through the business.

Just like with earnings, you want to be operating in companies that have free cash flow available to them. This means you don't want to see an 'N/A' value in the column that indicates the price to free cash flow figure (P/FCF).

Price to Book Value

Book value is a misunderstood term among a lot of investors. Put simply, it measures the value of all the assets the company owns minus the liabilities. In other words, if the business were liquidated today, how much would it fetch in a sale? In a real fire sale, these assets would be heavily discounted but book value is just a paper measurement.

You want a company to be selling for something close to book value or at a sector average figure. Comparing the PE to PB (price to book) ratios is instructive. Some companies that don't have a PE ratio can have a moderate or good PB ratio.

A high PB ratio indicates the company is being overvalued far too much and that it is likely to fall the minute the slightest adversity hits it. In contrast, a company selling at close to book value is a good candidate to increase its earnings down the road. This is because much like how the PE ratio can expand in value, PB can as well.

This boosts your earning potential on the stock. While it may not expand over your holding period when you trade the stock, having the potential in place is useful. After all, who knows when the expansion might occur?

These four ratios provide traders and investors with a good handle on what the earnings look like in a stock and how under or overvalued the stock price is with respect to earnings.

Leverage and Assets

Just like how free float accelerates the price increase in a stock, leverage does so as well. Leverage refers to the amount of debt that is a part of the company's capital. The more leverage it carries, the more sensitive the stock price will be to any news item or event that takes place.

Debt to Equity

This is a standard ratio that is looked at by almost everyone in the market. It is also one of the most misinterpreted. Conventional wisdom instructs investors to stay away from companies that leverage ratios over one. This indicates that 50% of the company's capital is funded by debt.

High levels of debt can be problematic for a company, After all, this debt needs to be serviced and interest payments place a huge burden on cash flows. However, debt also has its advantages. It can boost returns massively. Let's look at this via an example.

Let's say you have the chance to buy an asset for $200 and that this asset produces a return of $2 every year. That's a return of one percent. Not very great, is it? That's around what a savings account will pay you. However, through the intelligent use of debt, you can boost your returns in this massively.

Let's say you find someone who is willing to lend you $198 to fund this purchase. You invest just $2 of your own money in this deal. When you get paid $2 at the end of the year, your return on investment is 100%. After all, you've invested just $2. This represents your equity in the deal. The debt is $198.

Your leverage or debt to equity ratio is 99 which is eye watering but you can see how it has boosted your returns. It's turned a one percent return into 100%. The flip side of this situation is that it can go horribly wrong for you as well. If the investment declines in value to $198, you've just lost all of your equity in the deal.

In real life, you'll have to make interest payments to the lender as well. Therefore, you'll need to ensure that the rate of return on the investment is greater than the interest rate you have to pay. Your profit will be the difference between the two interest rates (what you pay versus what you get).

The same scenario applies to companies as well. If you were investing for the long-term, you want to stick to companies that have manageable debt to equity ratios well under one. However, when trading you want to look for companies that have high leverage.

This is because you've already screened for companies that are poised to move upwards. A higher leverage ratio indicates that the move in stock price (which is what the equity is worth) will move up to a greater degree than a stock that isn't leveraged. Much like our example, a one percent gain can be turned into 100% with leverage.

It can go wrong as well and you could see the stock move violently in the other direction. This is where risk management comes into the picture. You'll learn how to manage risk intelligently two chapters from now. For now, keep in mind that leverage is a good thing when trading over the short-term.

As long as you've run your screens correctly and are managing risk well, you'll stand to make outsized gains in your trading.

Current Ratio

The current ratio measures the state of the current assets versus the current liabilities. Current in this context means less than a year away. Current assets include things that can be quickly liquidated to produce cash. These occupy a separate section on a company's balance sheet.

They include cash, receivables and inventory. Cash is self-explanatory. Receivables or accounts receivables (AR) refer to payments that are owed to the company by its customers. Inventory refers to the value of goods and products the company has on its books. Any manufactured products or work in progress products are included in this figure.

Current liabilities are those debts that are coming due within a year. These are short-term interest payments and other debt that is due for payment. Companies regularly issue bonds as a means to finance their operations. Bonds require the company to pay a minimum amount of interest to the bondholders. When the term of the bond expires (or matures), the company needs to return the principal to them.

This places a huge cash burden on the company when the time comes. Having an adequate amount of cash or current assets on hand to address this is a good thing to look for. The current ratio is calculated by dividing the current assets by the current liabilities.

You want the assets to be a decent multiple of the liabilities. A ratio of one implies that the company is barely scraping by. Stay away from such companies since you never know what might push them over the edge. When they do move into the red, their stock prices will go tumbling and it'll be hard for you to get out of the stock position quickly.

Goodwill and Intangibles

These two line items are particularly important when it comes to looking at penny stock fundamentals. Goodwill will most likely not be present on a small company's balance sheet.

When one company buys out another, it usually pays a premium over the current stock price of the smaller company. This premium needs to be accounted for somewhere and goodwill is what handles this. It's an accounting creation. Companies with a large amount of goodwill tend to grow through acquisition and this is a dangerous strategy over the long-term.

After all, a string of poor purchases can mean massive impairment to asset values. When it comes to penny stocks, these are small companies to begin with so the notion that they're growing through acquisition is absurd. This is why goodwill won't usually be present. However, if you do encounter it you now know what it means.

A penny stock company that has a high amount of goodwill is not a safe bet to trade. A single impairment will result in a massive fall in percentage terms since these companies don't have too many assets to begin with.

Intangible assets are another place where a lot of bad quality assets are hidden and whose values can be inflated. An intangible asset is something that cannot be valued through regular monetary means. For example, what is the value of the trademark that Coca-Cola or Ferrari have?

Those names are clearly valuable. Slap another sticker onto a Ferrari and it instantly decreases in value. How does one measure this? Well, this is where intangibles come into play. The company's accountants estimate this figure and include it in the intangibles section of the balance sheet.

While it makes sense for Coca-Cola to have substantial intangible assets, a penny stock company that has anything more than 10% of its asset value locked into intangibles is just misleading or living in its own dream world.

Patents also come under intangibles and many tech startups that sell for pennies believe they're changing the world through their systems. These companies regularly inflate asset values to ridiculous levels in the name of owning disruptive patents and other Silicon Valley nonsense.

Such companies are usually found out sooner rather than later and you don't want to be anywhere close to the scene when this happens. It's best to simply steer clear of them, no matter how promising a rise your screens point to.

Special Events

Special events refers to all kinds of events that deal with a company's future and outlook. These usually include many different things such as spin offs, mergers, lawsuit settlements, earnings announcements, dividend announcements and so on. These events can be tracked through the news surrounding the company.

Such events produce huge interest in the stock and as a result the average trader stands to make a lot of money by betting in the right direction. Many traders tend to position themselves ahead of time, but this is not a viable strategy unless you happen to be intimately familiar with the stock.

Instead, track the company through the news and aim to take positions in situations that will result in outsized gains. This way, even if you enter at a higher than normal price you'll stand to make huge gains. Lawsuit settlements are particularly helpful in this regard.

Other special events include the announcement of a new product or some new patent. There is no limit to the number of special events a company can experience. Identify the ones that you're comfortable with when paper trading and trade these events when you go live.

Chapter 6:

Technical Analysis

Technical analysis is what most traders rely on when it comes to making market decisions. Having said that, technical analysis isn't infallible. Most traders quit trading in disgust because they keep losing money by following technical signals. As I mentioned earlier, the point is for you to understand that all signals have inherent probabilities of being right.

Your aim should be to be right most or even some of the time. Risk management is what makes you money when you happen to be right. In this chapter, I'll be spotlighting two extremely profitable technical trading strategies that you can use. The first one is a simple moving average crossover strategy.

This will seem simplistic to you at first glance and truth be told, it *is* an extremely simple strategy. I'm highlighting this because you don't need overly complex strategies to be successful in the markets. All you need is a strategy that you understand and ally that to strong risk management.

That is how money is made in the market and it's what you need to do in order to be successful. So stop looking for complicated ways of making money and stick to the simple methods. The less moving parts your strategy has, the easier it will be for you to implement it.

Moving Average Crossovers

As I mentioned earlier, moving average crossovers are both a screen as well as a trading strategy. The premise behind it is simple. When the faster EMA crosses the slower EMA, this is a bullish signal. You should enter on the close of the bar where the crossover occurred.

You can place your stop either below the slower EMA or below a relevant support level. A bearish signal would occur when the faster EMA dives below the slower EMA. Given that we're operating in penny stocks, it's best to stay away from bearish signals.

Most traders fail at implementing a crossover strategy. This is because they use it in a rote fashion and take every single crossover that they see. This is not how you're supposed to trade. As with candlestick patterns, you need to take the prior market context into account.

Trends

EMA crossovers work best in situations where prices are ready to breakout. Such situations can be tricky to spot. More often than not, the right signal will put you in on the first bar of a new uptrend. However, how can you identify such situations?

It's instructive to look at what such situations are not in order to understand that they are. For starters, you don't want to use this strategy when there isn't a huge force behind a trend. In such situations, prices are not heading decisively in any particular direction. As a result, if you enter into a position, you'll find that the stock won't move very far and the counter trend move will stop you out of your position.

Another scenario where you don't want to use this strategy is in large sideways moves. There is a caveat to this which I'll address shortly. Large sideways moves in the market usually indicate that a trend is about to come to an end. The tricky part is that these moves are usually so long that it takes a while for the new trend to emerge from it.

In the earlier portions of these moves you don't want to be using a crossover strategy. This is because prices will move up and down repeatedly and the EMAs will throw multiple signals. Instead, you want to look for signs of the sideways move coming to an end and a new bull trend forming.

The easiest way to spot this is to look for the presence of higher lows. This occurs when swing lows repeatedly form at higher levels. It indicates that the bulls are pushing prices higher and are overcoming the bears. When this happens, you can begin to consider crossover entries once more.

This is the only time when you ought to be looking at crossovers in sideways moves. The rest of the time, stay away from them. Figure 8 below shows how crossovers can get you in at the right time on bull trends. INUV has been in a range for a while and the two EMAs crossover one another repeatedly.

The faster EMA is the smooth line while the slower EMA is the stepped line. Notice that once INUV beings making higher lows, the signal right after the second higher low results in a huge upswing. As such, it correctly predicts the start of the bull trend. This is pretty much how you should trade crossovers.

Figure 8: Crossover Before a Bull Trend

The presence of the higher lows is what drives the decision to enter. All crossovers prior to this would have resulted in either a loss or a break even at best thanks to prices swinging around up and down.

You can play around with the intervals of the EMAs as you like. In this example, I've used five and 20 as the intervals for the fast and slow EMAs. However, you can use other combinations. Just make sure that there's a large enough gap between the two intervals. If this isn't the case, you'll be tracking just one EMA effectively.

Also take care to not make your slow EMA too slow. If the interval between your fast and slow EMA is too much then you're going to receive a bunch of false signals. For example, the 5 EMA will regularly cross over the 50 EMA. While some of them will work out, for the most part you're going to receive false signals. The slow EMA is just too slow to be reactive.

This is the case even when the intervals are close to one another but both EMAs are slow. For example, if you use a 30 and 50 EMA interval, both of these are far too slow to be of any use to you. Your aim is to capture quick upward moves in stocks. Using intervals of this size will not help you do this in any way.

Take your time paper trading EMA crossovers. Once you have them memorized and understand the perfect market conditions to deploy them in, you'll find that you'll make a lot of money with them. The key is to hold on for as long as possible. After all, if you're going to get in early on the trend, it pays to hold on for the entire extent of the trend.

This will reduce your need to keep buying the trend and you'll earn huge profits with every trade of yours. Some traders choose to exit when the fast EMA crosses the slow EMA from above. This can be a valid exit strategy. A better one is to simply wait for the trend to show signs of exhaustion and to burn itself out.

This way, you'll be exiting at the top or close to the top of the trend. Reading exhaustion signals requires you to understand the correlation between price and volumes.

Volumes and Price Correlation

I've already mentioned how volumes play an important role in stock market trading. It offers a direct insight into how the bulls and bears are distributing themselves in the market. By reading the signs correctly, you'll be able to align yourself with the side that is more likely to win out.

Having said that, it can be difficult to read the correlation correctly all the time. This is more of an art than a skill and it requires a lot of practice. It isn't impossible but it isn't a strategy that most traders can successfully implement. If you find that the strategy doesn't work for you, you can stick to crossovers and use candlestick patterns to find great entry opportunities. Fundamental screening might also work for you.

So what does volume and price correlation involve? Simply put, you want to see whether volumes match price action. Let's say you see prices increase strongly. How do you know whether this move will last for a long time? If there are a large number of traders behind the move then it's more likely than not to last for a while. A small number of traders will result in the move exhausting itself.

The best way to determine the number of traders in a move is to simply look at the bottom of the price chart where volumes are indicated. Some charts color code these volumes with red indicating volumes on a down day and green indicating volumes on a rising day. My advice is to ignore these colors and have single colored bars indicating volume.

This will prevent any biases forming in your mind. It's important that you do this because reading volumes and correlating them to price is extremely subjective. A bias will exaggerate what's truly going on in front of you. Before we get into the business of looking at charts, there are a few simple concepts to keep in mind.

The first is that increasing volumes always indicate strength. As I mentioned above, you want strong moves in the market to be backed by equally strong volumes. Typically, you will see volumes drop off when the market goes sideways. This is because most trailers in the market don't bother with sideways moves.

After all, you can't make money if the market doesn't move. However, sideways moves provide a lot of clues as to which direction prices will move in once the sideways move ends. If you see a sideways move with low volume after a trending move with high volume, it almost always results in prices continuing higher once the sideways movement ends.

Within the sideways move itself, you can compare the relative volumes behind the upswings and the downswings. This will give you a good idea as to the relative distribution of orders. The idea is to look at a chunk of bars and analyze the relative volume. Don't fall into the trap of looking at the volume that accompanies each and every bar.

I've mentioned exhaustion already. This occurs at the end of a trend where the trend traders push hard against counter trend traders and end up overextending themselves. They burn themselves out in the process and provide you with an ideal counter trend trading entry. There are a few tell-tale signs of exhaustion.

The first sign is massive volumes. I'm not talking about an increase but an explosion in volumes. The trend traders put their entire might behind this move so you should see a huge increase when compared to the volumes that existed previously.

The second sign to look for is the size of the exhaustion bars. These will be large in size, much larger than the ones that preceded them, and will sometimes have a large tail (in the case of a bear trend exhausting itself. Wick in case of a bullish exhaustion). This tail indicates that the bulls are ready to come back into the market and are already pushing back.

Don't expect prices to immediately go the other way. Sometimes, they'll continue to drift in the direction of the trend before turning back downwards. Let's look at a few charts to understand how climaxes and volume to price correlations work.

Figure 9: Selling Climax/Exhaustion

Figure 9 shows a bearish exhaustion or selling climax in INUV. This is not a traditional bearish exhaustion. Here, the volumes are huge (as indicated by the arrow) but the price bars are small in size. The volume is the key here.

The stock has been in a downtrend for a while and has shown indications of bullish strength increasing. This is not shown in the chart but printed as a large sideways movement. Further indications that it is a valid climax can be seen in how volumes increase as right before the arrow.

They keep increasing but prices don't go much lower. From a supply and demand perspective what's happening is that these selling orders are being absorbed by the buyers. Finally, the bears exhaust themselves and prices immediately spring up higher. In this case, you could have entered on the close of the climactic bar with a stop below it, at some distance away.

Once you've entered that position, all you'd have had to do was hold on until you spotted a buying or bullish climax. What does this look like? Figure 10 below is the same as Figure 8. This time, I've superimposed the volume over the chart without the EMAs. Notice that volumes spike even before the climax but these aren't valid signs of exhaustion.

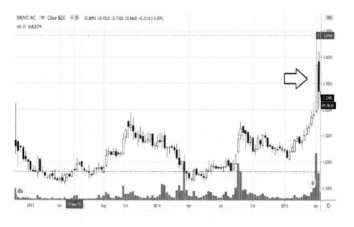

Figure 10: Bullish Exhaustion

The term exhaustion implies that some force has been expended before the event. In the cases where volumes exploded without a significant rise in prices, this is not the case. The bulls have not had a chance to expend any force let alone exhaust themselves.

You might think that Figure 9 had similar scenarios where volumes increased without price expansion and why that was considered exhaustion. The difference lies in what happens prior to these events. Again, remember that when evaluating trading signals you should take the entire picture into account, not just a few bars.

In that case, a bear trend had been on for a while and the bulls had shown signs of interfering with it. We were expecting them to step in soon and for the trend to end. Once volumes increased and prices stopped moving down, it was reasonable to conclude that the bear trend was ending.

Here, this is not the case in the middle of the chart. We see volume spikes within the sideways move but the bull trend hasn't even begun as yet. So how can the bull possibly exhaust themselves? Once the trend begins, we see the tell-tale sign of an explosion in volume with a correlated increase in the size of the price bars.

Notice the long wick on the climactic bar followed by the huge decline in prices right after it. Exiting during either one of these bars is the right move. Setting exhaustion aside, you can use volume to price correlation to enter a position before large moves. Pay closer attention to the sideways move in the chart in Figure 10.

Notice that towards the left of the chart, volumes are uniformly low. This portion of the chart is mostly bullish in nature and occurs soon after the climactic bearish move in Figure 9. Despite the selling climax, the bulls aren't ready to step in yet. As the sideways move develops, notice that the downward moves have greater volumes associated with them.

I'm not referring to individual moves but to entire chunks of the chart. The downswing from around $2 to less than a dollar has pretty good volumes in it. This means the bears are still around. However, notice that the dynamic changes after this swing is complete. Price moves up slowly and then volumes increase dramatically as prices swing upwards.

This is the first time bullish moves have produced such volumes. Prices swing downwards to form a higher swing low. This was the point after which we decided to look at EMA crossovers. Notice how volumes disappear completely in this downswing.

Compare the volumes here to both the bullish move that preceded it as well as the first half of the sideways move. You can see how bearish strength has evaporated. All of this means the bulls are ready to start pushing prices upwards and this is precisely what occurs.

Two different systems but both of them provide the same message and both of them get you in on the trend before it explodes.

There is a caveat to reading values in this manner. Special events such as news announcements or earnings announcements will distort the price to volume relationship. You should be aware of any such scheduled announcements or of the probability of such news being released before you decide to speculate in such stocks.

If you look at historical data and spot some sort of abnormal price to volume move, it's probably the effect of a news announcement. Given how subjective this method is you should take the time to fully practice this method with multiple instruments and market sessions.

The toughest part of this method is deciding on stop placement. The easiest way to do it is to place your stop below the closest relevant sr level. This way you'll be insulated from moves that go counter to what you expect. When trading this way, your holding times will also be a lot longer than what normal traders can expect. On average, you can expect to remain in a position for at least a week; maybe even more.

This is why paper trading is so important. It helps you figure out the various metrics in your system and also lets you know what you can expect in terms of trade performance. If such long holding times aren't suited to you, then you can try trading candlestick patterns or crossovers. These strategies usually have short holding times and you can exit according to risk management rules as well.

Speaking of which, it's now time to dive into the other pillar of successful trading. A lot of traders focus only on the technical aspects of trading but ignore their risk completely. As you're about to learn, this is a huge mistake.

Chapter 7:

Risk Management

Risk management is a large topic and, truth be told, an entire book can be written about this. Unfortunately, no one would ever read it because most traders have no idea that it even exists! The fact is that successful traders employ successful risk management systems.

Without a good risk management system, all you have in a bunch of entry signals. If you re-examine all the material you've learned thus far, you'll realize that all you've learned is a bunch of entry signals. This is what a lot of technical and fundamental analysis aims to do.

The problem occurs when traders think that this is all they have to do. It isn't the entry but the exit that determines how much money you make or how much of a loss you take. You can have a picture perfect entry signal that can go wrong. Worse, you can take this entry signal but exit at the wrong time and end up losing money.

Successful trading isn't about making money but keeping the money you make. Many traders are successful over a month or two but very few make money year in and year out. This is because they don't have systems in place that protect the capital or profits they've made.

Some traders take a few steps towards successful risk management but stop short of it due to either a lack of willingness to go the whole way or plain ignorance. For example, quite a few new traders use stop losses and stick to them no matter what. This is a good habit to have.

However, stop loss orders are not the only thing that risk management is about. Instead, they're a small part of the larger picture. So what is risk management all about exactly and how can you incorporate it successfully into your trading? It all begins with understanding the markets well.

Most traders approach trading as if it were an exam in school. They view every trading decision as a pass or fail type of deal. They think that if they get enough trade decisions right, they'll end up making a lot of money. This is not how the market works. The truth is that you're never going to be 100% correct about your decisions in the market.

You're never going to be able to predict every single move in the market with perfect accuracy. There will be many times when you'll be completely wrong with your prediction. For example, you could spot a really nice crossover setup and have all the preliminary conditions in place. Prices could still drop downwards, hit your stop loss and continue upwards, leaving you with a loss.

These kinds of things happen all the time to traders. Newbie traders think they're being singled out by the market somehow and put this kind of behavior down to broker corruption or whatever else makes sense to them. Many of them switch between trading strategies every other week or so, in a hunt to get as many questions right on their trading exam.

They fail to realize that when trading you're dealing with probabilities. The patterns and systems you've learned thus far all have a good probability of succeeding. This doesn't mean you're going to succeed every single time. What you need to do is understand that it doesn't matter how often you succeed.

This is because being profitable in the market is a combination of two factors. How often you're right, and the amount of money you make when you're right (versus the amount of money you lose when you're wrong). These two factors create a band of profitability.

Average Wins Versus Average Losses

Let's say a trader wins just 30% of the time. If they place 10 trades, they lose seven and win three. Is this person a successful trader? Conventional and academic wisdom would say no, they're not. After all, how can anyone be successful when they're right just 30% of the time? If you were taking an exam in school, and scored that low, you'd fail that test.

However, in the markets this single stat is irrelevant. It is just one part of the profitability question. The other part deals with the average win versus loss. In other words, how much do you make when you're right, and how much do you lose when you're wrong.

Let's say the average loss the trader makes when they lose is R. If they manage to win an average amount of 2.5R on the three trades they win, they're making money. They'll lose 7R on the trades they lose and make 7.5R on the three trades they win. As long as they're making money, who cares how often they win or lose?

That's what trading really comes down to; the win percentage and the average win-to-loss ratio. The latter is also called the reward to risk ratio. These two exist in tandem with one another. If you modify one, the other moves as well and affects your profitability.

Let's say the trader in question is unhappy with making just a 0.5R profit over 10 trades. They decide to take their profits earlier. This means they win a larger number of trades but their average profit per win decreases because they're exiting sooner. Let's say their win percentage rises to 40% and their average win-to-loss ratio decreases to 1.5R.

In this scenario they lose 6R and win 6R. This has them breaking even over 10 trades. Thus, despite being right more often, they're actually making less money. Try telling this to a newbie trader who seeks the holy grail of trading that is the perfect indicator.

Such traders chase after 100% accuracy rates in the belief that being right is what counts. As you can see, increasing your accuracy rate means nothing if the average win-to-loss ratio doesn't keep up. What if a trader is right 80% of the time but their average win-to-loss ratio is 0.2R?

In this case, they lose 2R and win 1.6R giving them a loss of 0.4R. They would be better off with the earlier numbers where the trader was right just 30% of the time.

This relationship between the win percentage and average win-to-loss ratio is what underlies successful risk management.

Consistency

The key to keeping the money you make is to ensure that you consistently follow the principles that keep these two numbers in place. This means you need to execute your trading strategy consistently and take all of the signals you receive. It also means that you should keep R as consistent as possible.

Let's tackle the first issue. Consistency in execution is a by-product of following consistent principles with everything else. From the way you prepare to the way you approach your market analysis. It also has to do with the way you practice your skills and look to improve them.

Many traders assume that market success is all about memorizing a few entry methods and then copying and pasting them over and over again. This is not the case. The markets keep changing and your system needs to adapt with them. You'll find that the behavior of certain stocks will change over time. This is because the nature of traders operating in them will change as new people enter the markets.

It isn't just people that are entering but machines as well. I've already mentioned how most market making trades are placed by algorithms these days. There are hedge funds out there that are constantly analyzing the markets and building mathematical models to simulate future prices. They operate across different markets, searching for the tiniest of inefficiencies.

They operate on different time frames and have vast resources. You might think it's impossible for you to compete against them. This is true only if you try to play the games that they play. If you stick to your chosen strategies and use simple techniques to analyze and trade the markets, you'll be just fine.

The key for you is to be able to keep working on your skills and to master them. For example, you might find that the moment when the EMA crossover happens changes over time. Only someone who constantly observes and studies the market can manage to spot such behavior and change their strategies in time.

Being consistent means you follow the same preparation patterns before you sit down to trade. It means you take preparation seriously to begin with. Many unsuccessful traders roll out of bed and look at the markets trying to figure out where they can apply their strategies in a formulaic pattern. This doesn't work.

You wouldn't' show up to the workplace like this, so why would you think it would work when it comes to trading? Take the time to fully prepare and make sure you're on an even emotional keel before sitting down to trade. If you're trading discretionary strategies, then it's even more important for you to make sure you're emotionally balanced.

If you're having a tough time in your personal life, then this is not the time for you to try to make money in the markets. If your capital is composed of money that you cannot afford to lose, you should not be trading. This alone will prevent you from making so many of the mistakes that unsuccessful traders make.

These types of traders chase wins and try to exact revenge on the market for their losses. They lose a few trades and feel the need to get right back into the market to try to win those losses back. This results in them placing poor trades that don't fit their rules and even more losses follow.

A lot of risk management is qualitative. In other words, the state of your mindset is crucial for your success. If you're not aware of where your mind is or what thoughts are floating around within it, you're going to have a tough time making money.

You don't need to be a monk of some sort to become aware. Make a list of behaviors that you engage in when you lose money. Observe yourself and monitor your triggers. I'll give you a few tricks to prevent yourself from falling into this trap. However, you're the one that ultimately needs to prevent yourself from over trading or engaging in revenge trading of any kind.

A lot of unprofitable behavior in the markets can be nipped in the bud with the knowledge you've just learned. We default to the 'need to be right all the time' mindset with everything that we do. Reminding yourself that trading isn't about that goes a long way towards preventing yourself from losing your mental balance.

Here's a conclusion you can draw from what you've learned thus far about the nature of trading. If everything depends on probabilities and if the odds will play themselves out over the long run, there's no earthly reason for you to care about the individual results of a trade is there?

After all, the loss that you take right now is simply a part of your bigger picture odds. As is the win or series of wins you're experiencing. They're not huge events by themselves and these results will even out over the long run and will conform to your odds. For example, you could win five trades in a row and be tempted to think you're the greatest trader in the world.

However, if your system has a win rate of 30%, you can bet that over 1,000 trades, you're going to lose 700 times (roughly speaking). This is even more true when you consider a sample size of 10,000. Given this knowledge, does caring about five measly trades really matter?

Pat yourself on the back, but understand that a single trade, or even a handful of trades means nothing. You need to consider your results 500 or 1,000 trades at a time. That's how long it takes for your odds to play themselves out. Obviously, the same applies even for losing streaks.

Throughout all of this your task is to maintain consistency in terms of preparation and practice. Winning five trades in a row doesn't make you a great trader any more than losing five in a row makes you a terrible one. As long as you're executing rules and strategies that you know have an edge in the market, you'll be just fine.

This edge is developed in paper trading. Truth be told, paper trading is where you'll truly develop the skills to be a great trader. Live trading should be easy compared to it. I'll detail how you can go about doing this in a later chapter.

For now, let's move on to the second point with regard to consistency.

Risk Per Trade

You already know that consistency in terms of execution is important. From a quantitative standpoint, consistency in maintaining a steady level of risk per trade is extremely important for your profitability. This can be illustrated via an example.

Let's say you risk R on one trade, 2R on another and 5R on the third, thinking it's a great trade setup and that you wish to go all in. Let's assume your success rate is 50%. We have three trades here so let's assume the first two trades are winners and the third is a loser. Your reward to risk multiple is R (or one).

Over these three trades you would have ended up with a loss of 2R (lose 5R and gained 3R). If you had kept your risk per trade consistent at R, you would have ended up with a profit of R (lost R and gained 2R). By simply keeping your risk pre-trade consistent, you would have turned a 2R loss into a gain of R.

You might argue that if the 5R risk trade had turned a profit, you would have made lots of money. This is true only if you know the outcome of the trade beforehand. If you happen to know this, there's no reason for you to be reading this book!

A consistent risk per trade helps you remain in the band of profitability that your success rate and your reward to risk ratio define for you. If your R per trade changes, your reward to risk ratio changes with it and you can get kicked out of that band. Some traders think they'll average their R out over time.

In other words, if they've risked 5R in a single trade, they'll risk 0.55R over the next nine trades in a bid to bring their risk per trade back to R. The problem is they don't know which trade will go for a win and which one will go for a loss. They might end up winning all of those nine trades and only manage to break even or lose money.

It's best to not shift your R value when you trade. R should be fixed to a certain percentage of your account's capital. This brings us to another striking point with most traders. They keep their R consistent but fix it at a very high value of their account's capital. This leaves them extremely vulnerable to drawdowns.

A drawdown is an event that reduces your account's balance from its peak. Let's say you start off with $1,000 in capital, grow it to $1,500 and it then reduces to $1,200. The period between $1,500 to $1,200 is a drawdown. You will always have drawdowns when trading, it's a part of the business.

Your peak drawdown is the highest decrease your account experiences. In the previous example, if you manage to go from $1,200 to $1,600 and if your account then falls from $1,600 to $1,200 again, your peak drawdown is $400 (1600-1200). Peak drawdowns are important to track and minimize.

This is because if your account gets drawn down too much, you'll likely not be able to recover from it. This is because as your account balance keeps decreasing your risk per trade will decrease with it. If this happens, your reward amounts will decrease and it becomes a lot tougher to recover account value.

Some traders double their risk per trade in such circumstances in an attempt to recover faster. However, this doesn't work because you don't know which trade will be a winner and which one will go for a loss. A trader that does this is in a poor mental state and will likely lose thereby accelerating the speed with which they wipeout.

The best way to reduce the speed of your drawdowns is to risk a lower amount per trade. This way your account grows at a slower speed but when you hit a losing streak, you'll be able to recover a lot faster. When it comes to drawdowns, statistics suggest that traders who lose more than 20% of their money usually never recover (Pardo, 2011).

20% should be a figure that you shouldn't even sniff when it comes to your trading. Your aim should be to control your drawdowns to a maximum number of four or five percent on a monthly basis. If you violate this limit, you need to stop trading for that month. After all, not everyone is at their best at all times.

Even professional athletes have bad games and all they do is train for their sport. You too will have bad market days. By minimizing your chances of blowing up during the bad times you'll ensure you have enough capital to see you through the good times when you can really press home your advantage.

All of this begins with keeping your risk per trade a consistent percentage of your account. The exact percentage will be determined once you're done paper trading and can figure out the expected profitability of your system. Typically, novice traders should not risk more than two percent of their account per trade.

However, even this is a very high number and ideally you should not be risking more than 0.5% of your capital on a single trade. This might seem like a very small amount of money. On a $500 account, that's a risk value of $2.50. This is where trading penny stocks is so powerful.

With that amount you can still purchase five shares priced at $0.50. If this stock rises even to $2 or $3, that's a massive gain for you. Your account will grow exponentially and compound in size in this way. Just don't withdraw any of your profits once you begin to grow your capital. This will hurt your compounding, and reduce the maximum amount of money you can make.

Other Metrics

Aside from your risk per trade, win percentage, average win and average loss you should also track your maximum drawdown limit, your proximity to your monthly drawdown limit and your recovery time.

The recovery time measures how long you took to recover from the trough of the peak drawdown to the new equity peak in your account balance. You want your recovery time to be twice as fast as your drawdown time. A system that doesn't recover fast enough might not be robust enough to keep you out of trouble, if a long losing streak strikes.

In these scenarios, low success rate systems do a lot better. If you're winning just 20% of your trades, then your average win is going to be many multiples of your average loss. This means your losses will not add up to much in the face of a single win. In contrast, a deep drawdown in high success rate systems will result in a curve that is slower to recover.

However, with a high success rate system your drawdown should theoretically be shallow to being with.

Whatever the case is, make sure you capture all of these metrics in both live as well as paper trading. Make sure you journal all of your trades and capture all relevant information about them.

Your entry points, your stop loss levels, your reason for entry and a screenshot of what you saw prior to entry are minimum pieces of information you should be recording at all times. You should also record your mental state as well as your reasons for exiting.

Speaking of exits, you can target either your desired R level according to your profitability zone or an exit given to you by an indicator strategy (such as with the crossover). If you're choosing the latter, make sure it helps you fall within the profitability zone at a minimum.

Chapter 8:

Scaling into Live Trading

Now that you're well versed with the basics of the technical aspects of trading and the risk management aspects, it's time to put all of this together into a coherent trading plan. How are you going to go about establishing a successful trading business? More importantly, how can you act to ensure that your success will be inevitable?

For starters, you need to forget about trading live for at least six months. I know this seems like a long time, but six months spent refining your trading strategy will ensure years' worth of profits for you. So be a little patient and you'll reap the rewards.

Next, you need to develop a plan to learn your new strategies and even take some out for a test drive. After all, you're not going to be an expert right after you finish reading this book!

The best way to practice is to first begin by looking at static charts. Looking at live charts right from the beginning will only confuse and intimidate you. Instead, go back over prior price action and take a look at how prices moved and which strategies you could have employed.

If you've decided to use candlestick patterns then try to spot these patterns. Remember that the geometric shape isn't as important as the underlying order flow. Look at places where prices swung from forcefully and see if there are any patterns over there that you can spot.

Speaking of swing points, take the time to fully understand and identify support and resistance zones. You will need to understand how they work no matter which strategy you're using. It's very important that you understand how they work and also which ones are relevant.

By relevant, what I mean is that newbie traders tend to mark every single level on the chart. Look at the force with which price is currently moving and match that to the strength of the level. If you're using a strategy like the EMA crossover, you won't have to rely on support and resistance as much since you'll receive entries from the indicators directly.

However, it's a good plan to learn all about sr anyway. Think of it as being a tool in your arsenal that you can use at any time. Often, sr alone will alert you to trading opportunities ahead of indicators. In the long run your aim should be to enter trades using just candlestick patterns and sr zones. It takes time to build up to this level of skill so keep practicing whenever you get the chance.

It helps to set aside designated hours during the day to practice your trading skills. Don't think you need to set aside hours on end. If 15 minutes is all you have, then ensure you practice for those 15 minutes rigorously. Quality is what matters, not quantity.

The aim of these sessions is to familiarize yourself with the way the market moves and what price looks like on a chart. If you've never looked at candlesticks before, you should take the time to study them before moving onto patterns. Man traders skip this step and try to build strategies right from day one.

This is a mistake. It's a bit like jumping into a car for the first time and expecting to set a lap record around a racetrack. You'll only end up exhausting yourself or even worse, crashing the car. Take it slow and steady and you'll achieve success.

Once you're familiar with the way candlesticks behave, and have a good idea of how prices on different timeframes move in relation to one another, it's time to start paper trading.

Objectives

If you're carrying out a task, it helps to learn what kind of goals you ought to be chasing. Many traders sit down to paper trade but don't have any goals in mind. This causes them to run around blindly in the hope of finding some kind of indicator that will bring them a 100% success rate. As I've already mentioned, this is the wrong expectation to have.

Your paper trading regime should be structured. In this regard, you need to set realistic goals for you to target. The first goal to target is to learn your strategy inside and out. You might have some trading strategy in mind. Perhaps it comes from the ones you've learned in this book, some combination of them or even something you read elsewhere.

Whatever it is, this strategy will have a lot of moving parts to it. Your first objective should be to master these parts. You should be able to figure out an entry by simply glancing at the charts. For example, if you're going to be using a crossover system, you need to be great at figuring out when a sideways move is breaking down and a trend is about to start.

After all, using this strategy in sideways moves is the wrong way to do it. Take the time examining these moves and also look at trends. Are there any crossover opportunities that they present you with? Once a crossover does occur, you'll need to place your stop loss order somewhere.

Where will this go? Convention is to place it below a close by support level or below the bar you enter if it happens to be a large one. The exact location will depend on the price chart dynamics in that moment. It is important for you to test out different stop loss placement levels at this stage.

The objective isn't to check whether you would have made money or not. While that is the ultimate goal, focusing on it constantly isn't going to help you at this point. Instead, try to understand the various elements within your strategy. Is it a practical one? Do you need to enhance it in some way to make it even more effective?

More importantly, is it something you can see yourself running day in and day out? Time frames also play an important part here. You can trade penny stocks using the 60-minute charts or even the daily chart if you don't have a lot of time to devote to the markets. However, if you want quick action, you can dive down to the five-minute charts as well.

The pace of price action will be very fast at this level and most beginner traders will find it immensely tough. However, you should take all time frames out for a spin to see whether you can cope with the pace.

All this talk of time frames might prompt you to think which software will help you do all this? Ninjatrader is a great software to use for the stock markets. It allows you to replay market action over time and you can switch between time frames. The best feature of the software is that it allows you to replay historical market bars in real time.

You can replay the day's price action at night as if it's occurring live. This allows you to build your live trading skills in a safe setting without risking real money. There are some free online trading software programs, but none of these are as good as Ninjatrader. It will cost you money, but consider it an investment. You'll more than make it all back once you start making money.

Once you've taken a few strategies out for a preliminary spin, it's time to move on to the first phase of paper trading. This is the simulation phase.

Simulation

During this phase, your objective is to gather data on your trading system. You've chosen one that you think fits, and it's now time to figure out what kind of rewards you can make from it. Can you risk consistent amounts while trading it and still make money?

This stage builds not just confidence in your strategy but also your risk management skills. You should write down what your entry signals are and what your exit strategy will be. Will you exit at a pre-planned reward multiple (2R, 3R etc.) or will you look to the price chart/indicator to give you a cue? Note all of these down.

What role will sr play in your strategy? Write this down as well. Once you're relatively certain that you can spot the necessary price entry cues, it's time to simulate your trades. You will need to replay the market bars one at a time to place trades and determine your paper profits.

You can replay them at any speed you like. Some software allows you to run through an entire day's worth of price action in five minutes. If this is too quick for you, you can slow the pace down. Your objective is to place 500 trades. That sounds like a lot but you'll be done with it within a few weeks.

If you can place 20 trades every day, you'll be done with this exercise in less than a month. It's important for you to place these many trades because of the learning that is taking place. Remember, you're building your trading skills, as well as taking your system out for a spin. You need to learn all about its risk numbers and your ability to execute the strategy.

At the end of this 500-trade period, you'll have enough data to figure out how profitable you can be. You'll know the success rate of the system, as well as the average win-to-loss ratio. Make sure you journal all of your trades through screenshots and other relevant information as mentioned earlier.

Review all of your trades and take a look at whether you can boost its profitability. If you've been unprofitable at the end of these 500 trades, then evaluate whether you executed the strategy properly. Sometimes, even the easiest looking of strategies are tough to execute. So don't look at this as an indictment of your trading abilities. Instead, the strategy simply isn't suited to you. Move onto something else.

If you have been profitable, try to see whether playing around with the reward levels can increase profitability. Keep in mind that if you aim for larger rewards, your success rate usually drops. Also keep in mind that reducing the reward level sometimes boosts profits thanks to the win rate being boosted massively.

There's no set of guidelines I can give you here. Play around with the numbers and see what you get. If you're satisfied with the numbers, you have then you can move onto the next stage.

Phase Two

This second phase also involves paper trading but this time, you're going to be trading live price action in the markets. You won't be risking real money at this stage so don't worry. You can use Ninjatrader or you can sign up to a trading simulator that is available at various online sources.

By this point, you're well versed with your strategy and have a great idea of how the risk numbers work. You understand where you need to place your stop losses and where your rewards need to be placed. If you're still uncertain, then go back to the previous stage and make sure you cover these points in detail before advancing with this step. There's no point hurrying forward with things unless you've taken care of everything else that preceded it.

With demo trading, your objective is to be profitable. It doesn't matter how profitable you are. If you end up making a cent, then you're profitable. Your aim should be to be profitable over a period of six months at the very least. You don't have to earn profits every single month or week. This would be impossible.

Instead, you should aim to be profitable at the end of this rolling period. All the while you should ensure your risk parameters are kept in place and that you're executing your strategy successfully. Keep your risk per trade consistent and at the percentage of your account you decided previously.

Since you would have executed 500 simulated trades at the very least, you should have no problems doing this. If you find your discipline wavering and see that you're tempted to risk different amounts per trade then take some time to read the previous chapter again. Specifically, focus on why it's important for you to risk the same amount of money (percent of your account) per trade.

Demo trading opens an area of trading that simulation doesn't. This has to do with preparation. When simulating trades, the trader usually goes through a large amount of market data in a short time. With demo trading, you're observing the live markets and there isn't any way for you to speed things up.

This means you'll need to prepare for the markets prior to their opening and you'll have to monitor your actions in session. What I mean is, you'll have to observe your actions in session and make sure you're not distracted. Some traders get bored by the market and decide to spend time browsing the internet. Ask yourself whether a professional trader would ever do this.

Forget professional traders, would you ever spend time on the internet browsing websites at your own workplace? How long would it be until your boss walks up and has a quiet word with you about this? Treat your trading session time as a business and take it seriously. If you find yourself getting distracted, then consider using some technique such as meditation to refocus.

If you're far too distracted, then consider switching off and stepping away. If your mind isn't focused on the markets then you have no hope of earning a profit. Make sure you aren't disturbed or bothered in any way when you sit down to trade. Demo trading is also the ideal time for you to record your psychological state in session.

What thoughts are coursing through your mind and how are you reacting to various market situations? Are you getting bored with the market? Are you feeling stressed? Constant signs such as these indicate a possible timeframe mismatch.

During the weekend, you need to review all of your trades and your journal. Note how well you executed your trades and what your psychological state was. Reviewing your psychological state is just as important as reviewing your trade entries and exits. If you started beating yourself up over a few losses, what does this reflect about your mindset?

How well are you executing your risk management knowledge? Remember that individual results don't matter. Are you patting yourself on the back a little too much after a streak of wins? While this feels great, even this indicates improper understanding of risk principles.

Throughout this time you should be recording the relevant metrics of your trading system. These metrics have been listed in the previous chapter. Here they are once again:

1. Risk per trade
2. Average win-to-loss ratio
3. Peak drawdown amount
4. Peak drawdown time
5. Recovery time

These are the bare minimum in terms of metrics. You can also record the following:

1. Average stop loss size
2. Average time for winning trades
3. Average time for losing trades

These three metrics will give you a good idea of what your entries are like. If your average losing trade lasts a lot longer than your winning trade, then you're probably entering a few incorrect opportunities. Either that or your stop loss is too far away. Your objective should be to quickly have the market confirm that you're in a good trade.

Having said that, this doesn't mean you want your losing trade time to be somewhere near a second. A losing trade time that is so low implies you're trying to stop a runaway freight train and are getting run over. Look at all three of these metrics together to complete a picture of what your trading looks like.

A lot of traders find that winning trades tend to work out right from the start. At the very least, they don't go into the red by too much in the beginning. Examine price behavior right after you entered to see whether you can spot any patterns.

You will be tempted to conduct your reviews in a cursory manner and get them over with as soon as possible. However, the more time you spend reviewing your trades the better. Keep looking for patterns in your results and your trading will become a whole lot better.

It's also a good idea to record your trading session on video using software such as Camtasia. By doing this, you'll be able to observe yourself, and your actions, during the session. It might seem like overkill, but the more you invest at this time into your trading the better your live results will be.

Once you're profitable over a six-month period, it's time for you to go live. By this point, there will be close to no doubt about your ability to be successful in the markets. After all, you've spent a ton of time paper trading and will know your strategy inside and out. You will have the confidence of knowing that you've made money on paper over a six-month period.

All you'll need to do is repeat whatever you did over this time and you'll achieve the same results. Live trading might catch you out since your money is now on the line. If you think this is going to be a problem, begin by risking as little money as possible. Trade just one share if need be. You'll find that by minimizing your money risked in live trading and by repeatedly executing your process, you'll develop confidence to trade and risk the amount of money you had previously planned.

Chapter 9:

Seven Steps to Trading

Success

You've learned a lot of material throughout this book and now it's time to condense all of this into a list of steps you can take to achieve your trading goals. These steps are simply a recap of everything you've learned thus far. They're also a framework you can use to plan your trading goals.

Step One - What is Your Why?

This is perhaps the most important step of them all; why exactly are you looking to trade the markets? What do you hope to achieve from it? Many traders simply think "money" and move on. However, this is not a satisfactory answer. Sure, money is great but the fact is that most of us have a lot of troublesome beliefs about money.

Everyone grows up in different households, and we carry unsupportive beliefs about getting rich. You might think that you need to be corrupt or somehow dishonest to get rich. You might think you're unworthy of becoming rich and so on. These are deep-seated emotional beliefs and there's no reasoning with them.

These negative beliefs will also impact you negatively when you go through a tough period in your trading. You'll find that your losses will seem worse and wins won't matter as much.

To counter this, you need to dig deeper and find the true motivations behind your trading. Perhaps you want to provide yourself and your family a better life. Perhaps you want to achieve some standard of living, or retire early on your passive income, and trading is a means to achieving that.

Write down a list of things you wish to achieve with your trading and how it'll feel once you get there. Review this list constantly and keep it somewhere close by. Do this right and you'll never lack motivation.

Step Two - Educate

Whether you know it or not, you're already on step two. This is where you take the time to learn all about trading and the way in which it works. You need to understand that trading successfully is more than just figuring out fancy entry signals. It involves a lot more than that such as understanding risk management principles and understanding the various ways in which you can enter trades.

Technical skills are important, but they form a very small portion of the overall picture. Instead, successful trading is built on two legs. Risk management and technical skills. Risk management is what makes you money and ensures you won't lose money in the markets.

It ensures you risk the right amount of money all the time and that your rewards are in line with the risk you're taking. It takes time to truly understand these points. It's one thing to understand them intellectually, but it's entirely another to know them from experience.

It is the latter that counts. This is why paper trading is so important, since it helps you gain experience without risking real money. You get to take the market and your strategies out for a spin, without having to worry about losing any real money.

Step Three - Invest

While all endeavors require time investment, trading requires monetary investment as well. A lot of traders come to trading dreaming of turning $500 into millions. The exaggerated tales of gurus out there does them no favors and leads them to think that this is a realistic thing to aim for.

Instead, your aim should be to adopt a more realistic perspective of things. Look to earn money in a sustainable manner and look to execute the trading process intelligently. You can risk 100% per trade and earn a 500% return. However, you don't need me to tell you about the negatives of pursuing such a strategy.

You will also need to invest money into tools that will help you trade better. A high-quality simulation software program is a basic investment that you should undertake. Instead of looking at this as a cost, you need to look at it as an investment in your trading success.

Without this tool, your chances of trading successfully are very low.

Unsuccessful traders severely underestimate what it takes to be successful in the markets and this is why over 90% of all traders lose money within their first year of trading. In order to be successful, you need to do the opposite of what these people do. So, invest in your own success.

Step Four - Familiarize

Before jumping into simulation, you need to familiarize yourself with the market and learn how it moves. This means learning about candlesticks as well as any component portions of your strategy. For example, executing a volume to price correlation strategy requires you to fully identify what a buying or selling climax looks like.

It also requires you to identify what it doesn't look like. You'll always see volume spikes in a price chart but not all of these are valid climaxes or exhaustion. You should take the time to look at charts and identify the various ways in which markets move.

Can you correctly identify declining volumes and compare volumes between different market phases? Every strategy has its unique entry identifiers, and taking the time to learn these better is a no-brainer.

Don't be in a rush to begin simulating trades. Your first instinct will be to do this right after you finish reading this book.

Instead, spend some time (invest) familiarizing yourself with the various components of the market. Look at how the price spread works and observe when it widens and when it contracts for example.

Step Five - Simulate

This step has been explained in great detail in the previous chapter. Once you're familiar with the different ways in which your strategy works you need to take the time to simulate 500 trades. Do not shortcut this step. Some successful traders even simulate 1,000 trades, just to be safe.

In fact, if you were trading at an institution such as a bank or a hedge fund you'll need to prove yourself to be profitable over these many number of traders before you ever sniff live trading. You need to treat your capital with the same level of respect and importance that these institutions do.

During simulations, pay attention to executing your process. It will be tempting to go back and undo some of your bad trades or to replay them as if you were in an 'ideal' state. Don't fall for this trap. Remember the two pronged goal of simulation. It's to gather data about your strategy and to build your trading skills.

If you go back and modify your trades or shortcut the process somehow, you're training yourself to expect this when you go live. Needless to say, you can't undo things in live trading.

Step Six - Demo

This is the second stage of paper trading that you need to undertake. During the demo stage you'll be placid trades on paper but will be looking at the live market. By 'paper' I don't mean writing down prices on paper and assuming entries. You need to sign up for a demo platform through your broker or some other third-party vendor.

There are a ton of free market simulation software programs out there that allow you to view the markets in real time. Sign up for one of these and practice your skills. The reason writing prices on paper doesn't work is because you won't be taking the spread into account. The price you see on screen is delayed and isn't where the market really is.

Demo trading also gives you the opportunity to practice your event handling skills. Generally speaking, stay away from trading around earnings announcements or important economic announcements, such as interest rate decisions or political events such as elections.

Prices jump around all over the place in such times, and you should be very careful to avoid them at first. Once you've built up real skills in live trading, feel free to trade these events. Until you can successfully and regularly produce trading profits, don't bother trading events.

The only exception is if you've built a strategy around them. In this case, you should practice trading them. Typically, such strategies involve analyzing fundamental events. If you're trading technicals using special events, you're not likely to be successful because the market won't give you enough time to enter at a good price; after the event has taken place.

Step Seven - Track and Repeat

The final step is for you to track and repeat all of the things you've been doing in a live trading environment. If you've done everything correctly, the live environment should not hold any special challenge for you. Some traders might find increased psychological pressure and I've already discussed how you should handle such moments.

Understand that success is built during preparation and you should not look to shortcut this at any cost. Take the time to figure out everything before you jump into live trading. Doing things any other way simply doesn't make sense.

Conclusion

Trading holds the promise of spectacular profits, especially penny stocks, but you need to put in the work before you get into a position to realize them. Throughout this book, I've been talking about how important practice and risk management is. These also happen to be the two points that most aspiring traders miss completely.

They seek to jump into trading the minute they obtain some capital and usually end up losing all of it. As I mentioned earlier in this book, making money is easy in trading. Keeping it is another task entirely.

In order to keep the money you've made, you need to prepare for it much before you begin trading with live money. Successful trading often comes down to consistency. Consistency in terms of executing your strategy repeatedly no matter the market scenario as well as in terms of quantitative metrics such as risk per trade.

This helps you build a solid platform from which you can take more risks and explore other strategies. Do not underestimate the power of practice and simulation.

These two things, more than anything else, will go a long way towards ensuring your success.

As a final word on the subject, let me say that you don't need to trade every single day of the year in order to be successful. Take some time during the year to review your results and to take stock of where you're at. There will also be moments when you'll simply burnout.

The markets will always be there for you to return to. So don't think they're going to go away. It's more important for you to maintain your psychological makeup instead of trying to squeeze every penny of profits from the markets.

You have an exciting road ahead of you and I wish you the best of luck! Remember the reasons you're looking to trade and keep them at the forefront of your mind at all times.

Happy trading!

References

Bloomenthal, A. (2020, May 17). *What Are the Rules Behind the Delisting of a Stock?* Investopedia. https://www.investopedia.com/ask/answers/09/stock-delist.asp

Pardo, R. (2011). *The Evaluation and Optimization of Trading Strategies.* (1st ed., Vol. 1). John Wiley & Sons, Inc.

Pattern Day Trader. (2020, January 1). www.sec.gov. https://www.sec.gov/fast-answers/answerspatterndaytraderhtm.html

Rodriguez, D., & Rodriguez, D. (2016, December 7). *Why Do Many Forex Traders Lose Money? Here is the Number 1 Mistake.* DailyFX. https://www.dailyfx.com/forex/fundamental/article/special_report/2015/06/25/what-is-the-number-one-mistake-forex-traders-make.html

Made in the USA
Columbia, SC
22 September 2020

21343791R00098